KU-659-534

American Education in the Twentieth Century

A DOCUMENTARY HISTORY

Edited, with an Introduction and Notes, by
MARVIN LAZERSON

CLASSICS IN

No. 52

EDUCATION

TEACHERS COLLEGE PRESS
TEACHERS COLLEGE, COLUMBIA UNIVERSITY
NEW YORK AND LONDON

Published by Teachers College Press, 1234 Amsterdam Avenue,
New York, NY 10027

Library of Congress Cataloging-in-Publication Data

American education in the twentieth century.

   (Classics in education; no. 52)
   1. Education — United States — History — 20th century —
Sources.   2. Education — United States — Aims and
objectives.   I. Lazerson, Marvin.   II. Title: American
education in the 20th century.   III. Series.
LA209.A54   1987   370'.973   86-30147
ISBN 0-8077-2852-7
ISBN 0-8077-2851-9 (pbk.)

Manufactured in the United States of America

03   02   01   8   9   10   11

Foreword

There can be no denying that the tension between equality and excellence has been a central theme in the recent development of American education. On the one hand, there has been the persistent quest for ever higher academic quality, as knowledge and expertise have become crucial factors in economic growth and as education has become a key element in international competition. On the other hand, education in general and schooling in particular have increasingly been viewed as devices by which the historic inequalities associated with race, class, ethnicity, and gender can be countered and a more equitable society achieved. Indeed, the history of American education in the twentieth century has often been portrayed as a series of pendulum swings back and forth between the two commitments, with excellence dominating in the 1920s and equality in the 1930s, and with excellence again dominating during the post-Sputnik era and equality during the era of the Great Society. As Professor Lazerson makes clear, however, it is less the alternation between the two commitments than their continuing copresence in tension that has marked the history of American education. One need only note the most recent instance of that copresence, namely, the issuance in 1983 of *A Nation at Risk: The Imperative for Educational Reform* by the National Commission on Excellence in Education and in 1985 of *Barriers to Excellence: Our Children at Risk* by the National Coalition of Advocates for Students.

Professor Lazerson explicates the tension between equality and excellence in twentieth-century American ed-

ucation with incisiveness and sensitivity, beginning with
the well-known conflict between Booker T. Washington
and W. E. B. Du Bois over the proper education of black
Americans and coming down to the profound differences
in the recommendations of the so-called national school
reports of the 1980s. And he relates that tension to the
long-standing ambivalence Americans have displayed toward their schools and colleges, assigning them critically
important social tasks at the same time that they consistently find them wanting. The documents he presents and
the informed commentary he provides shed new light on
contemporary debates over educational policy — debates
that will surely persist over the remaining years of the
twentieth century.

LAWRENCE A. CREMIN

Contents

Acknowledgments

This volume owes a major debt to the Spencer Foundation, H. Thomas James, and Marion M. Faldet for their willingness to support my efforts to study excellence and equality in American educational history.

My colleagues at the Harvard Graduate School of Education provided that special collegiality so fundamental to scholarship and teaching. My thanks to Patricia Albjerg Graham, K. Patricia Cross, Harold Howe II, Sara Lawrence Lightfoot, and Jerome Murphy. To David K. Cohen, a special note of gratitude.

Linda Eisenmann and Michael Fultz provided trenchant criticism, Ellen Condliffe Lagemann offered wise advice. My students — John Ameer, Sandra Baxter, Margaret Dollar, Martha Elkins, Beth Gamse, David Gordon, Noel Ignatiev, Andra Makler, Barbara Miller, Lenore Piper, Nancy Rhodes, Donna Schroth, and Camiliaumari Of Wankaner — were generous with both advice and criticism.

Joseph Shivers was a model research assistant; Debbi Reed's secretarial activities went well beyond the call of duty.

Ursula Wagener and Jared Lazerson kept reminding me that the issues were important and that I should treat them with care.

Finally, recognition to five great teachers: Richard Streb, Richard Hofstadter, Robert D. Cross, Lawrence A. Cremin, and Oscar Handlin. This book is dedicated to them.

American Education in the
Twentieth Century
A DOCUMENTARY HISTORY

Introduction:
American Education in the Twentieth Century

Americans have had good reason to be proud of their schools. They have enrolled more youths (and, increasingly, adults) for longer periods of time than in any other country. A majority of 7- to 13-year-old children were enrolled in school in 1900; almost 100 percent of that age group was attending by the 1960s, and more than 90 percent of the country's 14- to 17-year-olds were enrolled in high school. In 1900, 7 percent of the 17-year-olds were high school graduates; more than 70 percent were graduates in 1970, and half of each year's high school graduates were enrolling in postsecondary schooling. Going on to college and beyond has become part of the life experience of substantial numbers of Americans. On an extraordinary range of measures, America's egalitarian ethic has found fulfillment in its schools.

Yet during this same century, when American educational successes have been so outstanding, schools and colleges have been subjected to withering critiques — for failing to provide educational opportunity to all, for being unable to eliminate illiteracy, for democratizing at the expense of academic standards, for failing to teach useful subjects, for being too costly. Each success has seemingly been paralleled by an equally angry complaint.

The tension between pride and criticism has been a central feature of American education in the twentieth century. It reflects the desire to make schools all things to everyone. They are avenues of social and economic mobility whose primary purpose is to enhance equality of opportunity. Egalitarian aims lead to an emphasis on policies to improve access to education, more equitable distribution of resources, and curricula and pedagogies adapted to individual needs. A competing view of schooling stresses meritocratic standards. Thus it emphasizes selectivity and the academic quality of the educational experience and de-emphasizes the school's egalitarian responsibilities.

Still another set of expectations stresses the resolution of social problems. Americans have been peculiarly intent on trying to resolve social dilemmas through educational programs. Immigrant assimilation becomes translated into immigrant education. Economic and labor market problems lead to a focus on work training programs and the transition from school to work. Alcohol and drug use, automobile accidents, and adolescent sexuality all become the schools' responsibilities. As educational purposes become all-embracing, the schools are left in the unenviable position of being criticized both for not doing enough and for doing too much.

It is thus impossible to study American education without recognizing the tension between pride and high expectations, on the one hand, and intense criticism and disappointment, on the other. That tension is part of the enormous investment Americans have in their schools; as long as we care about education, pride and criticism and consensus and conflict will coexist. The important historical questions are how have the expectations taken shape and with what effects.

Part 1: The Transformation of Education, 1900–1929

The turn of the century was an extraordinary moment in American history. Industrial growth had made the United States the world leader in industrial production. Between 1890 and 1920, 18 million immigrants entered the country; perhaps even greater numbers moved within the United States from rural areas to cities, from the South to the North, from the East to the West. In 1920, for the first time, the census reported that more than 50 percent of the population lived in urban areas; many cities were populated more than 50 percent by immigrants and the children of immigrants. The United States was becoming an urban, ethnically diverse world power.

Technological and organizational changes were modifying the ways Americans worked and lived. Large industrial factories and the mechanization of agriculture created new working environments. Managing production and distribution, the growth of labor unions, and the development of managerial and office work placed a premium on service and organizational skills. Typewriters, telephones, and the establishment of accounting procedures accelerated the demand for secretaries and office workers. Electricity, the telephone, trolley and rail lines, the automobile, and marketing innovations like department stores and the Sears Roebuck catalogue were altering consumption and recreational patterns (Kantor and Tyack, 1982).

These changes and the tension that resulted from them underlay the emerging debate over the purposes and practices of American schools. How should school systems be organized to ensure the efficient delivery of services?

What values should be taught and to whom? How could schools best prepare youth for new job requirements? What should higher education's responsibilities be?

During the nineteenth century, American education had responded to these questions primarily by expanding. Although conditions still varied at the end of the century, the systemization of schooling was remarkably successful. Public taxation, enrollment of almost all 7- to 12-year-olds, standardized curricula, graded schools with students roughly the same age in a single classroom, and a lessening of the religious conflicts that had once sharply divided American education were all widely accepted (Kaestle, 1983).

Success rarely led to unanimity, however. Nowhere was this more apparent than in the vigorous debate between Booker T. Washington and W. E. B. DuBois. Although focused on the education of black Americans, the Washington-DuBois debate raised issues central to the education of all Americans: What kind of schooling best promotes educational opportunity, economic achievement, and democratic citizenship? Washington, the founder of Tuskegee Institute in Alabama, was the leading black spokesperson on education. His message articulated themes long prominent in American schooling: The school's primary purpose was to inculcate those moral values—thrift, sobriety, and industriousness—that enhanced achievement and character, and this was best accomplished by teaching vocational skills and "the everyday practical things of life" (Harlan, 1983). [Document 1]

DuBois also believed that moral values and practical skills should be taught in school. But he was critical of the one-sidedness of Washington's proposals. DuBois argued that education for blacks ought primarily to be directed toward the higher education of a "Talented Tenth" who would become "leaders of thought and missionaries of culture," exceptional individuals who would lead their people from second-class citizenship to equality. Charging that Washington would delay the rights of citizenship until blacks proved their worth, DuBois claimed that political equality and equal educational opportunity should be guaranteed to black citizens. The advanced education available to whites belonged equally to blacks (DuBois, 1903). [Document 2]

The issues so starkly drawn and vehemently debated by Washington and DuBois—the school's role in moral education, the teaching of vocational skills, equal educational opportunity, and the purposes of higher education—were fundamental to twentieth-century education. They were especially important early in the century as American education both coped with the thousands of children from diverse backgrounds flooding urban schools and sought to provide improved educational services to sparsely populated rural areas. Using words like efficiency, rationality, continuity, and impartiality, coalitions of lay reformers, businesspeople, and educators reorganized American education. They attempted to remove education from politics by centralizing and professionalizing educational administration, by separating school boards from local politics, and by consolidating rural school districts. They developed accountability procedures and IQ and standardized tests to measure abilities and learning, supervise teachers, and keep track of costs. Worried about the diverse effects of ethnicity—the perils of pluralism—schools added civics courses and night schools, Americanization programs, and, in some cities, "steamer classes" to prepare immigrant students for regular class-

rooms. Health and nutritional services, playgrounds, vocational guidance, and psychological testing further extended the schools' responsibilities. And, to ensure
competence and efficiency, university professional education training programs were established (Tyack, 1974;
Tyack and Hansot, 1982).

To an extraordinary extent, these efforts changed the
structure of American education. School boards declined
in size, superintendents of schools gained authority over
their systems, professional training programs for educational administrators proliferated, and school systems
took on a number of social service activities. Yet the
changes were incomplete and controversial. Schools remained open to politics; "old boy" networks of promotion and patronage stayed strong. Social services reached
only a small proportion of students. It proved impossible
to systematize the learning process and measure the outcomes of teaching in ways that the reformers had hoped.
The organizational reforms also brought conflict. Rural
villages and small towns fought efforts to consolidate
their schools. Ward politicians challenged the removal of
schools from their domain. Ethnic groups resisted the
derogatory implications of assimilationist policies. Catholic
parochial schools, often based on national allegiances —
Polish, Ukrainian, and Irish — grew at an extraordinary rate. Teachers worried about the role of supervisory
personnel and the centralization of authority. The grand
designs invariably had unforeseen consequences (Wrigley,
1982; Olneck and Lazerson, 1980; Katznelson and Weir,
1985; Reese, 1986).

Among those most affected by the attempts at change
were teachers. Few individuals articulated their concerns
more insistently than Margaret Haley, the charismatic
leader of the Chicago Teachers Federation. Haley's or-

ganization of women teachers was the most prominent and the most militant teachers' union in the country. Haley charged that school bureaucracies undermined teachers' initiative and professionalism by making them "automatons" expected to "mechanically and unquestioningly" perform their duties. Because, Haley argued, "the atmosphere in which it is easiest to teach is the atmosphere in which it is easiest to learn," the diminution of teachers was an attack on learning itself (Haley, 1982). [Document 3]

Across the United States, the teachers Haley hoped to organize were overwhelmingly female, usually young (because many stayed in teaching only a few years and were forced to resign once married), raised and educated close to where they taught, and insecure in their professional identities. For many, the issues were immediate: low salaries, exacerbated by women being paid less than men, and elementary teachers less than high school teachers; job insecurity, because most teachers were on annual appointments; and coping with the vicissitudes of daily classroom life. When teachers did organize, they focused on salary increases and tenure. When they were in their classrooms, despite the growth of teachers' colleges, they discovered themselves pretty much on their own (Urban, 1982).

Faced with schools and classrooms barely sufficient to accomodate the upwards of sixty students facing them, teachers stood in front of rows of desks bolted to the floor, textbooks in hand, and taught by lecturing or asking students to recite individually and in groups. The course of study was clearly set out. Classroom behavior was highly regularized, with a time and place for everything (Cuban, 1984).

Pedagogical reformers sharply criticized these behaviors. Often drawing on John Dewey's belief that children were naturally eager to learn and that teaching should begin with the child's interests and experiences, they attempted to reconstruct both the curriculum and methods of teaching. Seeking to apply his ideal of the school as a wise and loving family and of the teacher as a guide to learning, Dewey opened the most famous alternative school of his time—the Laboratory School of the University of Chicago. There, between 1896 and 1903, gifted teachers implemented such concepts as education as growth, the integrated curriculum, and the school as an embryonic community. In particular, Dewey's view that the school's obligation was to provide students with the knowledge, attitudes, and skills to engage in effective citizenship forged a crucial link between education and democracy (Dewey, 1916). [Document 4]

The belief that educational quality and educational opportunity were essential to citizenship was also transforming American higher education, especially in the public universities that had been growing in size and popularity since the late nineteenth century. Influenced by German models of research and teaching, caught up in the trend toward specialization of knowledge and the preparation of professional experts, and continuing a tradition of undergraduate teaching and *in loco parentis* responsibilities, universities began to define themselves as having three commitments—research, teaching, and service. One of the most powerful statements of this trend appeared in 1904 when Charles Van Hise, the new President of the University of Wisconsin, proclaimed his intention to make all of the university's expertise widely available so that "the sons and daughters of the state" would have the opportunity to study all forms of human knowledge.

"Nothing short of such opportunity is just," Van Hise argued, "for each has an equal right to find at the state university the advanced intellectual life adapted to need" (Veysey, 1965; Oleson and Voss, 1979). [Document 5]

The "Wisconsin Idea" that higher education would pay off—to society through the practical application of research and to the individual through occupational mobility—ensured higher education's growth and a new emphasis on utilitarian outcomes. There were, however, opponents to this view. Many denominational colleges retained their allegiance to religious values. The select liberal arts colleges for men and women continued to support the primacy of intellectual stimulation and character training. They also curbed admissions, in part to retain their elitism in the face of democractic expansiveness. The defense of the liberal arts and the college as "a place of the mind" found eloquent advocates, like Alexander Meiklejohn, President of Amherst College, and Robert M. Hutchins of the University of Chicago (Horowitz, 1984; Synott, 1979). [Document 6]

That was not, however, how higher education was coming to be defined. During the 1920s, with public universities and junior colleges leading the way, college enrollment increased from about 8.5 percent of the 18- to 21-year-olds to almost 12.5 percent of that age group. Students (and their parents) increasingly viewed college as a way to get ahead. As a working class father in Muncie, Indiana, explained in the mid-1920s, "I don't know how we're going to get the children through college, but we're *going* to. A boy without an education today just ain't *anywhere!*" (Lynd and Lynd, 1929, p. 187). To accommodate these expectations, the colleges and universities expanded the range of course offerings. Van Hise in 1904 boldly spoke of courses of study in languages, literature, history, political economy, pure science, agriculture, engineering, architecture, sculpture, painting, and music. By the 1920s, however, that list seemed narrow, considering the programs in law, medicine, business and commerce, home economics, dentistry, nursing, social work, pharmacy, and education that were available. At the same time, "college life," a blend of extracurricular, personal, and social activities, was becoming the most prominent feature of undergraduate education (Levine, 1986; Rudolph, 1977; Fass, 1977).

The transformation of higher education was apparent in the rise of professional schools. Through the nineteenth century, aspiring doctors, lawyers, engineers, and teachers had tended to learn their skills through on-the-job practice and apprenticeships. At the turn of the century, new demands for scientifically trained experts and the desire by some to make access to their professions more difficult led to efforts to increase educational and certification requirements. The most successful effort occurred in the preparation of doctors. Aided by the 1910 Flexner Report, a blistering critique of medical education, American medical schools became affiliated with research universities and teaching hospitals and began to require two to four years of college attendance for admission. The Flexner Report affirmed that higher education was becoming crucial to gaining access to the professions and to middle class occupations more generally (Lagemann, 1983; Bledstein, 1976). [Document 7]

Changes in high schools were even more dramatic than those affecting postsecondary education. Nineteenth-century secondary schools were small and unstandardized; often they were little more than a grade or two added to an elementary school. Since most youths left school at around age 12 or 13, such schools rarely received much interest. The informality of college admission policies meant that going to college did not depend on high school graduation. Not until the last quarter of the century did it even become clear that school districts could use tax monies for secondary education.

Between 1900 and 1930, however, the high school changed from a relatively minor institution that enrolled 10 percent of the 14- to 17-year-old population to one that enrolled well over half of that age group. Young people were both pushed out of the labor market and attracted into schools, as technology eliminated traditional youth jobs and created new jobs for adults and as adult immigrants and rural migrants entered urban labor markets. Increases in families' discretionary incomes meant that adolescent children were better able to stay in school, while child labor and truancy laws made it more difficult for young people to get jobs. Increasingly, colleges dropped the more informal methods of granting admission and began to require high school graduation. With more youths staying in school, the high schools had, by the 1920s, become the home for a new culture—the adolescent peer group (Krug, 1964, 1972; Kett, 1977; Cohen, 1985).

The growing importance of the high school was affirmed strikingly by the report of the Commission on the Reorganization of Secondary Education in 1918. Commonly referred to as the "Cardinal Principles," the report contained the message that mass secondary education had to be based on the practical results of attending school. The primary question was the usefulness of any school activity in contributing to the seven cardinal principles of education: health, command of fundamental processes (basic literacy and numeracy), worthy home membership, vocation, citizenship, worthy use of leisure, and ethical character. Conspicuous by its absence from the report was any mention of the high school's responsibilities to advanced knowledge, to learning for its own sake, or to the extension of one's mental capabilities. [Document 8]

The Cardinal Principles gave legitimacy to the dramatic changes that high schools were then undergoing. Paralleling the shift in higher education toward utilitarian outcomes, secondary schooling was also to be defined by practical results. Of these, none was considered more important than training for occupations. In the first three decades of the century, the vocational education movement achieved enormous popularity. Vocational education represented a shift from earlier traditions of schooling that stressed work habits and skills like ciphering and penmanship as useful to occupational success to an emphasis on more direct, systematic training for occupations. The new expectation was summarized by the president of the Muncie, Indiana, school board: "For a long time all boys were trained to be President. Then for a while we trained them all to be professional men. Now we are training boys to get jobs." The large enrollments of girls in rapidly expanding commercial education courses like typing and stenography revealed that vocational expectations were also applicable to girls (Lazerson, 1971; Lazerson and Grubb, 1974; Kantor, 1987).

In addition to its appeal as job preparation, vocational education was viewed as a way to curb a host of social and economic ills, from countering a shortage of skilled labor and reducing labor strife to eliminating high school dropouts and opening avenues of upward mobility, thus enhancing equality of educational opportunity. The movement, which reached its high point in 1917 with the passage of the Smith-Hughes Act providing federal funds for vocational training, resulted in vocational courses becoming a basic feature of the high school curriculum. Although vocational training courses never attracted as many boys as the reformers had hoped and were more attractive to girls through commercial education than the reformers had expected, the vocational educational movement reinforced the view that schooling's primary obligation was to pay off.

By the end of the 1920s, then, American education had been transformed from its nineteenth-century antecedents. Bureaucratic forms of organization and a heightened focus on efficiency, accountability, and measurement had taken hold. Youths spent more time in schools than ever before, and while in them created powerful communities of peer groups. The high school itself was being integrated into an educational ladder that began in elementary school and extended through college and professional schools. Universities emphasized research and service as primary justifications for public support. Professional certification was increasingly becoming dependent on extended years of schooling. Schools had taken on vocational purposes that made preparation for occupations a central concern. And a new term had emerged – equality of educational opportunity – that was used to describe programs and curricula adapted to individual needs, thus justifying vocational courses, ability grouping, individualized teaching, and electives.

Many of these themes were summarized in *Middletown: A Study in Modern American Culture* (1929), a remarkable study of Muncie, Indiana, during the mid-

1920s by Robert and Helen Lynd. Comparing the high school of the mid-1920s with that of 30 years earlier, the Lynds found major changes. In 1889-90, a Muncie high school student chose between two four-year courses of study, the Latin and the English program; the primary difference between them was whether the student took Latin or not. The total number of courses given in any year was twenty. In 1923-24, a student chose from one of twelve different courses of study—the General, College Prepatory, Music, Art, Shorthand, Bookkeeping, Applied Electricity, Mechanical Drafting, Printing, Machine Shop, Manual Arts, and Home Economics. The number of courses offered that year was 102 (Lynd and Lynd, 1929, pp. 191-192).

The Lynds also found that the vocational preparation courses had become "the darling of Middletown's eyes," that patriotism was a central concern, and that the extra-curriculum dominated school life. Although the city had few immigrants, the schools, at the state's urging, portrayed an America in need of constant citizenship training—the need to teach patriotism, American heroes, and American ideals. The extracurriculum of athletics, clubs, sororities and fraternities, and dances and parties attracted adult as well as student interest. The high school's athletic program in particular held the community's attention. In 1890, there were no high school athletic teams; in the mid-1920s, the basketball season produced a frenzy of excitement within and outside the school. While girls played some sports, their primary responsibility was to cheer the boys on. Club activities were more evenly distributed between the sexes; belonging to the most important clubs established a youth's status. [Document 9]

Like most Americans, Middletown's citizens lauded their schools. The large numbers enrolled and the range of curricular and social options seemed to provide youth with the essence of democracy—access, choice, and an education suited to particular abilities and interests. But, as the Lynds discovered, there were limitations. Educational opportunities in Middletown were shaped by one's social class and gender; had the Lynds studied Philadelphia, Atlanta, Chicago, or Los Angeles, they would have found opportunity limited by race and ethnicity. Middletown's laudatory message about education was also constrained by doubts, something Middletown's teachers understood. The young, unmarried women who taught in Middletown's schools were paid the same wages as were retail clerks. They lacked status and were rarely asked to participate in any major city activity. The schools were important, receiving about half the city's budget, but, the Lynds found, the teachers were "nonentities." They had become part of the paradox of American education: The schools were important, but the teachers in them were not.

Part 2: Continuity and Change, 1930–1941

The 1930's Depression hit Americans hard. Never before had so many suffered economic upheaval or had so many been unemployed. Many Americans doubted the efficacy of government and of themselves. When the Lynds returned to Muncie in the mid-1930s, they found a community "facing both ways": "A city living by the faith that everyone can and should support himself . . . had to confess that at least temporarily a quarter of its population could not get work. . . . A city committed to faith in education as the key to its children's futures has had to see many of its college-trained sons and daughters idle, and to face the question as to what education is really worth" (Lynd and Lynd, 1937, pp. 487–488).

That the Depression would affect education was inescapable. Cities and states suffered 20 to 33 percent declines in overall revenues in the early 1930s. Since public school expenditures were typically the largest of a community's costs, many school systems were virtually immobilized, with the poorest states and rural areas suffering the most. Nationwide, teachers' salaries dropped by 14 percent between 1929 and 1934. After decades of expansion and the buoyancy of the 1920s, night classes, summer schools, playgrounds and recreational programs, kindergartens, music and art activities, programs for the mentally handicapped, physical education, guidance, and vocational education were cut, and a continuing war over "fads and frills" was waged. Forced out of the labor market, increasing numbers of youth stayed in high school, leading to larger class sizes. American educators had to contend with management and teaching in an era of declining resources (Tyack, Lowe, and Hansot, 1984).

Retrenchment modified the politics of education. The dictum that schools and politics did not mix and that education was "above politics" took a back seat to the reality of political mobilization. Educators joined "Save Our Schools" coalitions to protest the dismantling of programs. The National Education Association increased its lobbying activities at the federal level. Teachers' organizations lobbied state legislatures to expand state aid to education, to pass teacher tenure and certification laws, and to consolidate rural schools and finance school transportation. The lobbying was often successful. During the

1930s, the proportion of local school budgets supported by state governments almost doubled, from 17 to 30 percent (Peterson, 1985, ch. 9; Mirel, 1984).

The situation of teachers was anomalous. Many joined the political efforts, but they rarely received community support for doing so. While activists like George Counts of Teachers College, Columbia University, called for teachers to engage in a "social reconstruction" of American society, most teachers defined themselves as professionals whose responsibilities were limited to the classroom. [Document 10] Although salary reductions, threatened layoffs, overcrowded classrooms, and the lack of teaching materials made life difficult, wholesale firings rarely occurred. Behind classroom doors, teaching practices remained similar to those of earlier decades. Lectures and recitations of textbook materials continued to predominate, and teachers, as sociologist Willard Waller pointed out, were very much constrained by the social mores of the communities they taught in and the organization of the schools (Waller, 1932). Still, the politicization of education during the 1930s brought more teachers into teachers' organizations and politics than ever before.

While the Depression had a mixed effect on teachers and teaching, it brought to the fore questions about the quality of teacher education. At the beginning of the 1930s, two-thirds of the nation's elementary school teachers had two or less years of postsecondary schooling; only 10 percent had completed four years of college. A comprehensive, six-volume *National Survey of the Education of Teachers* published by the U.S. Office of Education in 1933 found that "American public schools were taught predominantly by young, unmarried women with little teaching experience." Schools were unable to hold teachers beyond a few years; many of those who taught were only a few steps ahead of their students in both age and educational attainment. The situation was worst in rural areas and in schools for black children. Many teacher education programs lacked rigorous training in academic subjects and provided limited exposure to classroom practice. Whatever else it was, teaching was not a professional occupation for which young people received systematic training and engaged in as a long-term enterprise. [Document 11]

The Survey's recommendations reflected its authors' assessment of the problems: States should require a minimum of four years of college for elementary and secondary school teachers. Special attention should be given to upgrading the requirements for teaching in black schools. Equalization of educational opportunity required equalizing the preparation of teachers. Tenure and in-service programs should be extended. While recommendations like these were never fully implemented, over the course of the decade teacher education and certification requirements were greatly strengthened, the result of effective lobbying by teachers' organizations, the more general rise in college attendance, and a greater emphasis on credentialing. By the end of the decade, college degrees were becoming the standard for all teachers.

The curriculum too was subject to pressure for change, nowhere more so than in social studies. The political controversies of the 1930s pushed the social studies curriculum toward the teaching of social efficiency and personal adjustment and into courses on "the problems of democracy." Efforts to teach the virtues of the local community occurred in Middletown and elsewhere, and efforts to introduce coursework in interpersonal relationships proliferated (Lynd and Lynd, 1937, pp. 237–238; Franklin, 1986). More controversial were curriculum reforms that stressed the dilemmas of American life, as appeared in the report of the American Historical Association's Commission on the Social Studies (1932) and in the widely used social studies textbooks of Harold Rugg. During the 1930s, Rugg's texts on American civilization were used in school systems that enrolled nearly half of the students in America. The texts combined a variety of disciplines to explain American society, often raising questions about the free enterprise system and the existence of inequalities. While the 1930s opened up greater possibilities for such questioning, at the end of the decade Rugg's books came under heated attack for putting the problems of America too much in the forefront. In 1938, the texts sold more than 289,000 copies; in 1944, sales were 21,000; over the next decade they would virtually disappear (FitzGerald, 1979).

The most widely heralded attempt to change the curriculum came in 1933, when the Progressive Education Association persuaded some 200 colleges to waive their regular undergraduate admission requirements for selected high schools. Twenty-nine schools eventually participated in "The Eight-Year Study," most with already established reputations for innovation. Nineteen were private or university-related laboratory schools, ten were public high schools. The assumption was that, freed from the restrictions of standard college admission requirements, the schools would be willing to experiment with their curricula. Although the schools diverged in their practices, most adopted a core curriculum combining social studies and English courses that were team taught and focused on students' perceived needs. In a Des Moines, Iowa, public

high school, the twelfth-grade course was originally divided into two parts — American Problems and Practical
Problems of Living. Over the next few years, the focus of
the experiment shifted "from subject matter to pupil
needs as the criteria for the selection of content." The
shift compounded the difficulties of choosing curriculum
materials that simultaneously met state and local curriculum requirements, the expectations of teachers about subject matter, and the students' desires and needs (Aiken,
1942). [Document 12]

The Eight-Year Study did not alter the secondary
school curriculum; many of the participating schools re-
treated to what they had traditionally done. But more
important than the immediate effects of the experiment,
the curricular emphasis on perceived problems of living
and on students' needs paralleled a more general shift in
curriculum throughout the nation. The notion that practical utility and student-centered concerns ought to be
central to schools, a view that had emerged so forcefully
in previous decades, became in the 1930s the dominant
ethos of American education.

Concern over the transition between high school and
college, as found in the Eight-Year Study and the introduction of the Scholastic Aptitude Test by the College
Entrance Examination Board, had a certain logic. The
virtual elimination of the job market for youth during the
Depression accelerated the trend toward staying in high
school through graduation. Whereas 29 percent of the
nation's 17-year-olds were high school graduates in 1930,
51 percent were graduates in 1940. Nonetheless, large
numbers of young people still left high school before
graduating, and many graduates could not find work.
Somewhere between one-fifth and one-third of the country's 16- to 24-year-olds during the 1930s were both out of

school and out of work. Many faced long periods between the time they left school and the time they found full-time employment.

The inability of these youths to find jobs focused attention on issues of drift and alienation. As a major survey of 13,000 young people in Maryland, *Youth Tell Their Story* (1938), phrased it, "The gap which now exists between school and employment is reaching ominous proportions" (Bell, 1938). One outcome of this concern was greater stress on the ways that schools could more adequately prepare youth for work. Despite the Roosevelt administration's disinclination to fund educational programs directly, Congress extended federal financing of vocational education, originally established by the Smith-Hughes Act of 1917. Vocational guidance took on new prominence, as studies invariably urged providing young people with information and guidance about occupations. A comprehensive survey of high-school-age youth in New York State concluded that "large numbers of boys and girls on the point of leaving school either have no vocational plans or have plans which are quite out of line with their own demonstrated abilities and with opportunities for employment." Youth seemed to agree; the majority of those surveyed in New York reported that they would drop out of school if they thought staying would not improve their vocational chances. [Document 13]

The problems of unemployment were not equally shared by all youths. For blacks in the rural South and in urban centers, for Hispanics in the Southwest, and for Native Americans on and off reservations, the impact of the Depression, added to the long-standing problems of poverty, was devastating. In 1931, one-half the black children in the South were not in school; three-quarters of those enrolled were below the fifth grade. Per pupil expenditures were $15 a year, compared with a national average of $80. Surveys consistently found that black schools were meagerly financed, with poorly trained teachers, inadequate school buildings, and substantial gaps between the provisions for white and black children. Urban school systems systematically segregated black students. In the most comprehensive study of the decade, *Special Problems of Negro Education* (1939), a report to the President's Advisory Committee on Education, black educator Doxey A. Wilkerson harshly condemned the systematic lack of support of black educational institutions, from elementary school through college. Going beyond the early debate over the kind of education blacks should have, Wilkerson articulated the failure of American education to live up to its promise of equality of educational opportunity (Anderson in Kantor and Tyack, 1982). [Document 14]

Despite the inequities, black Americans continued to seek educational opportunities. School attendance by blacks increased at a rate double that of whites during the decade. The percentage of black youths in high school doubled and graduation rates tripled. Illiteracy declined enormously. For Southern black Americans, education was a means to get ahead; as a 12-year-old North Carolina girl told sociologist Charles Johnson, "If you get a heap of schooling you get plenty of jobs when you finish." [Document 15] In the North, blacks organized boycotts against segregated schools and fought to eliminate prejudiced textbooks and to gain more access to adequate vocational education programs. At the same time, the National Association for the Advancement of Colored People began legal strategy against segregation and the doctrine of "separate but equal" that would eventually bring it to the *Brown v. Board of Education* Supreme Court decision in 1954 (Franklin, 1979; Homel, 1984; Kluger, 1976).

The existence of poverty, unemployment, and the limited educational opportunity that was so much a part of black Americans' lives was emblematic of the inequalities Americans faced during the Depression. The New Deal never developed a comprehensive approach to eliminating those inequalities. Nor did it establish an articulated federal educational policy, in part because President Franklin Roosevelt believed that educational responsibility should remain at the local level and in the states. Rejecting repeated overtures by groups like the National Education Association to provide federal funds for schools without restrictions on their use, the New Deal evolved an educational policy focused on employment and relief rather than on schooling (Tyack, Lowe, Hansot, 1984; Fass, 1982).

Initially, the federal government provided funds to states as part of its work relief programs to hire teachers to keep the schools open, for school repair and construction, and for cafeteria, maintenance, and other workers. The Civilian Conservation Corps first established rural conservation camps for youth and then added literacy and vocational training programs. The National Youth Administration provided part-time work so that secondary and college students could stay in school, as well as offering jobs to school-age youths not in school. Finally, through its various work relief activities, the federal government supported preschool and adult literacy programs that employed over 40,000 people teaching 1.5 million people.

The New Deal's educational activities left an ambiguous legacy. While the federal government established the principle of intervention in a crisis, it did not define a legitimate and ongoing federal policy in education. Yet New Deal programs had a significant impact. Under federal sponsorship, an estimated 1.3 million adults, one-half million of them black, learned to read and write. Federal employment programs that allowed poets and authors to write, historians to do research, musicians, artists, and photographers to practice their crafts, and that used the radio and other media to communicate, significantly enlarged existing definitions of educational policy. The joining of social welfare to education similarly expanded educational responsibilities.

Perhaps most fundamentally, the New Deal's practices changed the definition of equality of educational opportunity. Before the 1930s, equality of educational opportunity was used primarily to justify varied educational programs based on students' perceived abilities or likely vocational choices. The assumption was that equality of educational opportunity meant giving each student access to a range of curricular choices. The New Deal modified this nearly exclusive emphasis on curriculum variety and choice by claiming that poverty significantly undermined educational opportunity. Federal involvement was based on the implied belief that for equality of educational opportunity to exist, inequalities rooted in class and race had to be attacked. The full consequences of that shift in thought would not become apparent until the 1960s (Fass, 1982).

Part 3: Educational Excellence in a Democratic Society, 1942–1963

World War II shifted and postponed many of the debates about education. Under pressure to provide child care for mothers needed in defense industries, the federal government passed the Lanham Act (1943), providing federal monies for day care centers. But, like the earlier New Deal legislation, the expectation that federal aid was for short-term crises meant that once the war emergency ended, the Lanham Act expired. The evacuation of more than 110,000 Japanese-Americans, many of them children, from Western states to "relocation centers" heightened the tension between egalitarian and democratic educational ideals and the reality of life in the centers. Youths left school to join the armed forces, disrupting educational programs. And yet, schools continued to function without significant changes, as August Hollingshead found in *Elmtown* (Grubb and Lazerson, 1977; James, 1985; Hampel, 1986). [Document 16]

With the end of the war, questions about how to improve educational quality and enhance educational opportunity surfaced with vigor. The Depression- and war-imposed halt to school construction, combined with a shortage of potential teachers, made school facilities and teacher supply the first order of business, especially as the first of the postwar baby boomers prepared to enter school. The problems pointed to some federal aid to education, in part because of the large amount of funding needed to improve overall quality of schooling and overcome the sharp inequalities in educational financing. Those inequalities had produced financial disparities that ranged from annual expenditures of $5,000–$6,000 per classroom at one end of the spectrum to $100 per classroom at the other.

Postwar proposals for federal aid to education quickly ran into roadblocks. Southern congressmen objected to any federal support that suggested equitable distribution between white and black schools; Catholic lobby groups, strongest in the large cities, opposed any federal aid that did not include private schools; and heated opposition surfaced over the prospect of federal control of local educational programs. Despite what seemed like a national sense that America's schools needed greater support, federal aid fell by the wayside. Although postwar affluence, the baby boom, and the remarkable growth of new suburbs made school building and the expansion of educational opportunity central to the American agenda after the war, until the late 1950s it did not appear that the federal government would be much involved (Ravitch, 1983, ch. 1).

There was, however, one significant modification of this position. When Congress deliberated providing opportunities for returning members of the armed forces, it was much less hesitant about federal aid. Fearful that returnees would be unable to find jobs and that the country faced a potential economic recession, as well as desiring to provide benefits for those who had served in the war, Congress passed the Serviceman's Readjustment Act of 1944, more commonly known as the G. I. Bill. The Bill provided a broad range of benefits, but its most lasting impact was in education. Veterans wishing to continue their schooling were given monthly living allowances and subsidies for tuition, books, and fees (Olsen, 1974). [Document 17]

The decision to provide federal aid to extend access to higher education was greeted with alarm by some, who feared a lowering of standards and overcrowding. Yet, the G. I. Bill was one of the most remarkable successes in American education. By the fall of 1946, more than a million veterans were enrolled in postsecondary institutions, almost doubling the college student population. By the time the Bill's benefits ran out seven years later, 7.8 million veterans had taken advantage of them.

In the process, the veterans changed the face of higher education. They did remarkably well, and colleges quickly testified to their academic achievement. The veterans introduced older students, often with families and young children, to college campuses, together with demands that housing, health, and other facilities be made available. Since the primary beneficiaries of the G. I. Bill were men—although benefits were available to both genders, almost 98 percent of the veterans were male—higher education became a more accepted route to careers for men than ever before. Perhaps most profoundly, the success of the G. I. Bill suggested that higher education should be considered a right, something to which Americans were entitled. By the mid-1950s, that sense of entitlement was increasing pressure to provide greater opportunities for larger numbers of American youth to attend college.

The impetus to college attendance given by the G. I. Bill soon turned into a tidal wave, as higher education went through an extraordinary transformation. Enrollments doubled between 1940 and 1960, from about 1.5 million students to 3.2 million; they more than doubled again during the 1960s as the full brunt of the baby boom hit the campuses. By the early 1980s, more than 9 million students were enrolled as undergraduates. The growth went considerably beyond the increased number of youths in the population, for greater proportions went on to college. In 1946, about one in eight college-age youths was in a postsecondary school; in 1970, the proportion was one in three, figures that underestimate the full impact because by 1970 greater numbers of older students were enrolling in college. Whereas approximately three of every ten high school graduates continued their schooling in 1950, almost five of every ten were continuing in 1970, and almost six of ten a decade later. For those who graduated high school, going to college was becoming a part of growing up.

With the increase in higher education, troubling questions about the purposes and practices of postsecondary schooling resurfaced (see Documents 5, 6, and 7). At Harvard University, a faculty committee issued a strong defense of the liberal arts and academic standards (Harvard University, 1945). A Presidential commission in 1948 asked, "How can higher education make society more democratic?" It responded by calling for a vast array of postsecondary institutions and the removal of all barriers to attending them. The ultimate educational goal, the commission concluded, was "an educational system in which at no level—high school, college, graduate school or professional school—will a qualified individual in any part of the country encounter an insuperable economic barrier to the attainment of the kind of education suited to his aptitudes and interests." Central to the goal of a democratic system of higher education, the commission believed, was a vast array of public community colleges that would guarantee access to anyone who desired it and that would serve as centers of community learning. [Document 18]

Growth in numbers reflected only one dimension of the democratization of educational opportunity. With state colleges and public community colleges the fastest growing sector of higher education and with private college tuition rates rising, the locus of higher education shifted from private to public institutions. In 1950, for the first time, half the college students were enrolled in public colleges and universities; a decade later, the proportion was up to 60 percent; by the early 1980s, it climbed to 79 percent. Under political pressure to serve their own constituents, states began investing heavily in postsecondary institutions. California led the way; its comprehensive master plan developed in the 1950s and 1960s proposed junior colleges, state colleges, and universities to provide postsecondary schooling to any high school graduate who desired it. At the same time, the multi-tiered system of higher education served to differentiate students by types of training, by qualifications, and often by social class and race. Higher education for all thus coexisted with sharp differentiations. While less comprehensive in their aims and practices, other states soon adopted higher educational policies similar to California's, further extending state responsibilities.

The shift in higher education to the public sector greatly expanded the university's responsibilities to serve the public good. In the postwar era, the "Wisconsin Idea" of research and expertise in the public interest—to expand the economy, solve social problems, and enhance national defense—and of providing an enormous variety of programs and courses became the defining characteristics of American higher education.

Federal aid to universities greatly expanded. Federal research and development funds in 1940 were about 15 million dollars; in 1960, the sum of federal expenditures for research and development was 1.5 billion dollars. By the mid-1960s, prestigious universities like M.I.T., Princeton, California Institute of Technology, Harvard, Stanford, and the University of Michigan were receiving large proportions of their budgets from federal sources.

Because federal support was not equitably distributed, the differences between the most prestigious schools and the others sharpened; because federal research money had become so highly desired, professors with access to research money became more desirable than those without such access. The result, in the words of the President of the University of California, was the creation of the "multiversity" (Nasaw, 1979, Part III). [Document 24]

The new prominence of the multiversity accentuated the vocationalization of higher education. Staying in school, initially through high school and then increasingly through college, was justified on the grounds that it was essential to occupational mobility. The imperative to stay in school to enhance economic achievement — which was supported by the certification requirements to enter the professions — widened the gap between those who completed four years of college and graduate school and those who left school after high school. While some Americans thought that one did not need a college degree to get ahead, most believed that continuing in school was essential. Indeed, so important had college attendance become that access to higher education took on greater political dimensions than ever before. The G.I. Bill was followed by political pressure to expand the state universities and colleges. Public community colleges grew at an enormous rate; national and state scholarships and loans aided enrollments. To these were added ferment over selective admissions procedures and agitation for more open access, all attesting to the importance attached to gaining entry to colleges and universities. Many Americans had come to believe that going to college was both a requirement for success and a right to which they were entitled.

Nor surprisingly, higher education's enhanced place in American society led to yet another look at secondary schooling. In the 1950s and 1960s, high schools became college preparatory institutions on a mass scale. If more and more students were going on to college, what should be expected of secondary education? If higher education was in the national interest, if automation and technology required new kinds of knowledge for occupations, what role should high schools play? These questions took on sharp dimensions in the 1950s as Americans grappled with a new kind of competition and conflict.

The Cold War with the Soviet Union was a shock to many Americans, who turned to potential enemies from within as the source of America's seeming vulnerability to the enemy from without. The schools became a target of those fears and frustrations, both because they were the potential battleground for the hearts and minds of the young and because they were expected to teach the technological and literacy skills to extend America's economy and protect its defenses (Ravitch, 1983, ch. 3).

These expectations led to two kinds of criticisms of the schools in the 1950s: first, that they were purveyors of questionable loyalty, leading to attacks on textbooks and teachers for being "soft on communism" and insufficiently patriotic; and second, that academic standards, particularly in mathematics and science, were too low to meet the demands of a technological economy and modern defense. The "crisis" came to a head when the Soviet Union launched Sputnik in October 1957. [Documents 20, 21]

One response to Sputnik was the National Defense Education Act of 1958 (NDEA). The Act's introduction attested to the perceived link between the schools and national security: "The security of the Nation requires the fullest development of the mental resources and technical skills of its young men and women." The sense of crisis removed the traditional roadblocks to federal aid to education—fears among Southerners that federal money would undermine segregation, opposition from religious groups angry at the exclusion of religious schools, and resistance to federal intrusion into local and state control of education. NDEA provided loans and fellowships to support science, mathematics, and foreign language study, which were deemed most necessary to the national interest, as well as funds for school construction and equipment. It gave students low-cost loans that could be substantially written off if they entered teaching. The first comprehensive federal educational legislation, NDEA also pointed federal support for education toward categorical grants, toward aid in support of specific federally mandated programs, and away from more general federal aid to be used by school districts as they wished. [Document 22]

NDEA was part of a broader set of activities initiated during the 1950s designed to increase both educational opportunity and academic quality. These included consolidation of small and rural schools to make it more efficient and economical to provide improved education programs, political mobilization in support of local bond issues for school construction and better classrooms, and vigorous teacher recruitment efforts to attract talented people into teaching (as well as efforts by teachers' unions to achieve gains in salary and working conditions). In an effort to improve educational quality, the Advanced Placement Program in secondary schools was instituted, which allowed students to take college-level courses. To attract meritorious youths, scholarship funds were greatly increased. The growing numbers seeking access to college, in turn, heightened competition to enter high status universities, while graduate programs for the professions expanded dramatically (Spring, 1976).

The pursuit of excellence and the expansion of opportunity took on innumerable manifestations, but few had quite the intensity of the curriculum reform movement of the late 1950s and early 1960s. Originating on university campuses, the curriculum movement sought to bring into the schools the most recent discoveries in subject matter and to combine them with new knowledge about learning theory. Substantial efforts were made to change the ways in which mathematics, the natural sciences, and foreign languages were taught, followed by similar, if less fully supported, efforts in the social sciences and language arts. "New" became the catchword of course programs, as curriculum reformers sought to alter subject matter and teaching that they believed were too often uninspiring, unintellectual, and insufficiently challenging for talented students.

The search for quality was variegated, but the curriculum movement took on certain common dimensions. Most important, the curriculum specialists believed that each discipline — physics, history, mathematics — had a particular cognitive structure that, when understood, would help students think like professional scholars. Discovering a few concepts — the "discovery method" — was considerably more important than covering the whole field and learning individual facts. In the "new mathematics," for example, understanding set theory and the way numbers were organized was considered more important than memorizing multiplication tables. Learning how a historian uncovers and uses evidence was more important than learning the dates of wars or the names of presidents. The emphasis on discovering underlying cognitive structures required "hands-on" learning; students would not learn about science, they would be scientists. [Document 23]

The curriculum reform movement possessed extraordinary vitality. College professors and teachers joined in summer institutes to write curriculum guides and textbooks and to produce films and audio-visual aids. Federal and foundation support for curriculum development, especially through the National Science Foundation, was the highest it had ever been. And yet the efforts produced mixed results. While new textbooks were written and many ideas about curriculum were modified, especially in the sciences, the dramatic transformation the reformers hoped for was not to be. Scholars, educators, and parents disagreed over what the essential "core" of knowledge should be. While mathematicians urged set theory on young students, teachers had little knowledge of set theory, and parents wanted their children to learn to count. Dubious about the quality of the nation's teachers, reformers had hoped to create "teacher-proof" curricula, but soon found that without teacher investment and commitment even the best material was unused or misused. Finally, and most profoundly, the nation's social and economic priorities shifted. The new curriculum movement was generated by Cold War concerns about the nation's scientific and technological capabilities. While the hope was that all students would benefit, primary attention went to the more talented ones. As the United States entered the 1960s, however, the demands of the disadvantaged and issues of equality of opportunity came to the fore, and with that shift, debate about educational purposes and practices changed (Lazerson et al., 1985, ch. 2).

Although they seemed to hit the national agenda unannounced, the issues of race, poverty, and equality of opportunity had been building since the mid-1930s. They took on new dimensions in May 1954, when the Supreme Court unanimously declared that "the segregation of children in the public schools solely on the basis of race" was unconstitutional. In stunning and simple language, the court had found that equal educational opportunity was an essential right, that segregation by law stigmatized the minority, and therefore that "separate educational facilities are inherently unequal." [Document 19]

Although the Supreme Court had already required the integration of graduate schools, *Brown v. Board of Education of Topeka, Kansas, et al.* hit Americans like a bombshell. Just after the decision, *Time* declared that no Supreme Court case had ever "directly or intimately affected so many American families." The Southern response varied from disbelief that much would come of *Brown* to outrage over the attack on the "Southern way of life." Some cooler heads suggested that the South could adjust to the Court's decision. In the North, a period of acceptance and satisfaction set in; few acknowledged that the Court's orders would soon affect Northern school systems (Kluger, 1976).

Implementation of the *Brown* decision was slow, in part because the Court waited a year before formulating its implementation order and then issued an ambiguous ruling. While calling for the admission of students on a nondiscriminatory basis "with all deliberate speed," the Court simultaneously emphasized that the complexity of desegregation required careful attention to local circumstances. More important, implementation was slowed by a policy of massive resistance in the Deep South. Yet, *Brown*'s impact should not be minimized, for it struck at the fundamental legal basis of racial discrimination. In making equality of educational opportunity a constitutional right, *Brown* propelled the schools to a central place in the civil rights movement. The decision was also controversial, even among those who agreed with its conclusion. The Court's claim that segregation was inherently unequal seemed to suggest that an all-black school could not be educationally excellent. "All deliberate speed" seemed too slow once it was determined that segregation was illegal. The Court's imposition of a federal mandate onto state legislatures and local school districts was taken as a rejection of the decentralized character of the nation's schools. And the Court's use of social science and psychological data to support its findings — that segregation harmed the emotional and psychological development of children — raised questions about the role of social science in developing legal principles and in deciding educational policy (Ravitch, 1983, chs. 4–5).

Brown quickly became an essential ingredient in the fight for racial justice. But it was soon upstaged by more direct action — a bus boycott in Montgomery, Alabama, in 1955–56 that brought Martin Luther King to national attention; the calling of federal troops to Little Rock, Arkansas, in 1959 to desegregate the city's high school; sit-ins by black college students in 1960 in Greensboro, North Carolina; "freedom rides" to desegregate facilities throughout the South; marches for voting rights; violence and near-violence at university campuses in Mississippi, Georgia, and Alabama; and the 1963 March on Washington. By the time of John F. Kennedy's assassination, civil rights had become the nation's primary domestic issue. Education was soon to be engulfed by it (Chafe, 1980).

PART 4: THE EXPANSION OF OPPORTUNITY, 1964–1980

When Lyndon B. Johnson assumed the Presidency in 1963, his initial agenda was civil rights, most importantly the passage of the Civil Rights Act of 1964, which guaranteed voting rights and, among other things, threatened to withdraw money from any federally funded program that discriminated on the basis of race, color, or national origin. The Civil Rights Act was followed almost immediately by the Economic Opportunity Act of 1964 (EOA), which, drawing on New Deal youth employment precedents, established job training programs and a Job Corps to train and employ poor youths. EOA also instituted community action programs that became the basis for Head Start, and it provided support for college work-study students and for adult basic education and migrant education programs.

But the centerpiece of federal educational policy in the 1960s was the Elementary and Secondary Education Act of 1965 (ESEA). Because the "war on poverty" was less a direct attack on poverty itself and more a series of programs to increase educational opportunity, ESEA was fundamental to it. ESEA, like EOA, grew out of two assumptions about poverty: first, that living in a culture of poverty taught the young attitudes and behaviors that inhibited their chances of breaking the cycle of poverty, and second, that children could be motivated to learn the skills necessary for school achievement. The expectation was, as President Johnson declared immediately after the

Act's passage, that greatly expanding "full educational opportunity . . . will help five million children of poor families overcome their greatest barrier to progress — poverty" (Jeffrey, 1978). [Document 25]

Labeled an "anti-poverty" bill, ESEA also circumvented the historic conflict over aid to private schools by adopting a "child-benefit" basis of federal funding: While federal money would be allocated to public agencies, the funds would be used to benefit eligible poor children regardless of whether they attended public or nonpublic schools. The heart of the legislation, the compensatory education programs of Title I, accounted for almost 80 percent of the 1.25 billion dollars initially allocated. Other parts of the Act provided financial assistance for library and instructional materials, centers for educational innovations, research and development, and strengthening state departments of education; at the same time, the Act disclaimed any federal intention to control the operation of local school districts.

ESEA was a historic event in that it consolidated the trends of the previous decade and established a clear-cut federal responsibility for educational opportunity and educational quality. Not surprisingly, a host of questions and controversies quickly followed. How would school districts use federal funds? Did equality of educational opportunity require racial integration? What degree of oversight should federal agencies have in the implementation of federally funded programs? How should programs designed to ensure equality of educational opportunity be evaluated?

These questions quickly became part of the controversies over the relationship of education to civil rights, equality of opportunity, and federal responsibility. They

achieved national attention beginning in the mid-1960s
with the publication of *Equality of Educational Opportunity* (1966), commonly referred to as the Coleman Report. Commissioned as part of the Civil Rights Act of
1964, the Coleman Report found that "the great majority
of American children attend schools that are largely segregated," that minority children start school academically
behind white children and their achievement levels worsen
compared with whites over their years of schooling, and
that family background has a much greater effect on
school achievement than anything the schools actually
do. Little of this was exceptional. But in developing the
argument, James Coleman and his colleagues suggested
that many of the most cherished assumptions about how
to improve schools — through better facilities, increased
expenditures, more training of teachers, compensatory
education, and improved curricula — had only a modest
effect on students' school achievement. Where schools
improved educational opportunities for minority students, they seemed to do so when some racial and social
class integration occurred — as long as white students remained in the majority. The Coleman Report's findings
seemed to distinguish between school improvement efforts that had little effect on eliminating the academic
achievement gap between minorities and whites and efforts to integrate the schools that had a more positive
effect on academic inequality. The outcome was a public
perception that schools in themselves made little difference to equality of educational opportunity, but that racial integration might make a difference. [Document 26]

The twin themes of racial integration and the limited
impact of school-based educational reforms quickly
dominated many of the debates about schooling in the

late 1960s and early 1970s. A report of the U.S. Commission on Civil Rights, *Racial Isolation in the Public Schools* (1967), found that racial segregation was increasing throughout the country, further undermining equality of educational opportunity, and that compensatory education programs were largely ineffective. These findings suggested still greater efforts at integration—through creating metropolitan school districts, magnet schools, and, most controversial of all, busing. Others went further, arguing that educational reforms could not change the basic structure of social class inequalities in American society. The initial evaluations of Head Start and Title I, the compensatory education part of ESEA, were negative, leading to still further doubts as to the efficacy of the educational war on poverty (Jencks, 1972).

By the early and mid-1970s, American education was in the throes of yet another crisis. The social reform activism of the previous decade, beginning with civil rights and compounded by controversy over the Vietnam War, had greatly intensified efforts on behalf of equality of educational opportunity. ESEA had been followed by a host of federal legislative and executive activites prohibiting gender discrimination in education, providing for federally funded bilingual programs, and greatly expanding the educational rights of the handicapped. [Documents 29, 30, 31] Each of these efforts was controversial, especially as gaps between expectations and implementation appeared. Social science evaluations raised doubts about the actual gains achieved by students in the new programs; even the most popular program, Head Start, was roundly criticized. But most compelling to policy makers and the public at large were the social conflicts that federal activism engendered and the financial costs of the new educational commitments. In school district after school district, education became highly politicized. Federal courts moved beyond the declaration that legal racial discrimination must end and demanded integration and evidence of special efforts to enhance educational opportunity. Traditional state and local methods of financing schools were challenged on the basis that unequal financing was unconstitutional. A 1963 Supreme Court decision, *Engel v. Vitale*, that forbade religious exercises in public schools became the basis of ongoing and intense division over the "secularization" of American education. Students gained the right to demonstrate and forced the introduction of more "relevant" courses into the curriculum. Community activists battled to decentralize school systems, create alternative schools, and expand resources devoted to ghetto classrooms. Teachers went out on strike. Violence over educational decisions appeared in a number of cities, and courts moved in to take charge of running the schools (Hampel, 1986; Lukas, 1985; Monti, 1985).

With the courts and federal government engaged in educational matters to a degree unthinkable a decade earlier, the politicization of American education between 1965 and 1975 was unprecedented. In part, the political struggles were so intense because the issues were among the most fundamental in American society: the disparities between the ideals of equality, liberty, and justice on the one hand, and the realities of discrimination and lack of opportunity on the other. Because the issues were so fundamental, the educational policies and politics of those years had to be controversial.

In these controversies, few events were more startling than the outbreak of violence on college campuses. In the two decades after World War II, higher education had been a remarkable success story. Public support for expansion to enhance economic growth and national defense, appeals to the ideal of equality of educational opportunity, and individual advancement into the professions gave higher education a luster it had never previously had. Although many Americans were ambivalent about the financial costs of college attendance, for an increasing number of parents, the desire to send one of their children to college became an integral part of family life. As the baby-boomers became youth — some 80 million of them were born between 1946 and 1964, altering the age composition of the population — they gained cultural and economic power that young people had never before possessed. Many middle-class youths assumed they were entitled to special attention, material goods, freedom, and a college education.

Beginning with the founding of the Student Nonviolent Coordinating Committee (SNCC) and Students for a Democratic Society (SDS) in 1960, and escalating into the Free Speech Movement at Berkeley in 1964, followed by incidents at Columbia, San Francisco State, Wisconsin, Michigan, Cornell, Harvard, Kent State, and Jackson State, to name the most prominent, students demonstrated in support of civil rights and against the Vietnam War. Their outrageous language and dress, open drug use, invasion of buildings, and finally violence and death produced shock waves. Many of the demonstrations occurred at the most prestigious universities; the demonstrators were among the most favored youth in the society. If those who were receiving the most rebelled, what had the efforts to build opportunity meant? It seemed to be a crisis unparalleled in the history of higher education. [Document 27]

What actually happened was confusing. Most students did not rebel, although many were sympathetic. A very small number engaged in violence. While most Americans opposed campus unrest, student demonstrations against the Vietnam War helped sway public opinion away from the war's escalation. Despite the demonstrations, college enrollments continued to increase. The clearest outcome was increased autonomy for students as colleges dropped their *in loco parentis* responsibilities, granted students greater decision-making responsibility on the campuses, and substantially reduced the number of required courses and gave students more control over the curriculum. As the civil rights movement lost much of its passion, as the Vietnam War ended, and as unemployment climbed, students returned to classrooms, leaving a legacy of confusion over the place of the university in American society and, it seemed, a legacy of hostility toward the young as overentitled, self-centered, and undisciplined.

The college rebellions of the 1960s and 1970s infrequently focused on the quality of teaching and learning. That was much less true in the elementary and secondary schools, where changes in pedagogy and curriculum were seen as central to the purposes and practices of schooling. Powerful attacks on ineffective and stagnant teaching, efforts to make curricula more relevant by offering courses of immediate interest to students (and teachers), attempts to eliminate racial and gender stereotyping from textbooks, alternative and free schools, community control, parental participation, decentralization of school districts, and the expansion of nonschool programs all testified to the determination to change how teachers taught and students learned. Of these reform efforts, few seemed to hold as much promise as "open education."

Its source was surprising—British infant schools. American commentators described students who learned when given freedom, classrooms in which forty youngsters noisily engaged in discovery centers while teachers moved among them to encourage their learning efforts. In sharp contrast to the mindless, dreary, authoritarian, and racist classrooms described by Jonathan Kozol, Herbert Kohl, Charles Silberman, and others, open education promised places of learning and places of joy (Kozol, 1967; Kohl, 1967; Silberman, 1970; Featherstone, 1971). [Document 28]

As a pedagogic panacea, open education proved illusive. Although open area programs were often interesting and well taught, the early optimism soon faded. Neglected were the warnings on how carefully planned and controlled the best British classrooms were. Educators could not simply turn students over to discovery and activity centers and presume that the students would naturally learn. Noise levels were unsettling to students, parents, teachers, and administrators. Letting students move at their own pace violated expectations of what had to be learned. By the end of the 1970s, the high hopes had faded; many classrooms were indeed more open or informal, especially for young children, but a revolution in teaching had not occurred (Cuban, 1984).

The waning of expectations and the growing criticisms of pedagogical and curricular reforms reflected more pervasive doubts about the efficacy of American schooling itself. As reaction to more than a decade of federal activism set in, with the experiments in educational and social reform found wanting and controversial, with the American economy on shaky ground, and with antagonism to young people high, Americans asked how much students were actually learning. The answer, a chorus of commentators declared, was "not much." As part of that message, opinion polls revealed that public confidence in schools was down.

The heightened publicity given to declining Scholastic Aptitude Test (SAT) scores between the mid-1960s and the early 1980s was one manifestation of the concern about school effectiveness. That the drop was taken as a measure of the health of American education was both ironic and logical. The irony lay in the origins of the SAT as a measure of aptitude, not school achievement; the SAT had been developed in the 1920s and 1930s as a way of measuring what the students were capable of, rather than what they had already been taught in the schools. The hope was that the SAT would expand opportunities for talented youth whose schools and teachers were less than adequate. The test was not supposed to measure school or teacher effectiveness. The logic lay in the prominent role the SAT had come to play in gaining admission to selective colleges and the realization that the test was actually a measure more of achievement — what was taught and learned — than of aptitude. As the scores appeared to go down, it appeared that so too had the quality of teaching and learning.

The causes of the decline were unclear, and there were later controversies over whether test scores had actually gone down. The decline was first attributed to the new populations taking the examination after the mid-1960s. The democratization of opportunity meant that greater numbers of nonwhite and poor youths, whose scores averaged less than those of white and middle-class youths, were seeking college admission. From the mid-1970s on, however, the decline also was attributed to a perceived drop in academic standards in the schools, the growth of "gut" courses, and the dominance of a live-and-let-live philosophy of education. But whatever the actual causes—and they were bound to be complicated and controversial—the decline in test scores was treated as a failure of academic excellence. [Document 32]

The politics of education at the end of the 1970s thus suggested that the educational activism of the previous decade left an ambiguous legacy. One form of that ambiguity lay in how to evaluate the efforts to increase educational opportunity. In 1960, fewer than two of five black youths graduated from high school, compared with two of three white youths. In 1980, the gap had narrowed to seven of ten for blacks and around eight of ten for whites. A greatly increased proportion of blacks entered and graduated from colleges. Women's opportunities had expanded; handicapped children were in classrooms previously denied them. Student academic achievement was aided by Title I and Head Start compensatory educational programs. Based on a substantial body of data, educational opportunities were more equal in 1980 than most Americans would have thought likely before the Second World War.

Yet the data were not all positive. Dropout and school achievement rates remained worse for blacks, Hispanics, and poor whites than for other groups. In the late 1970s, the situation began to worsen. The intensity of the conflicts over improving opportunity left many Americans questioning the worth of such efforts; the collective will to enhance equity lessened, even as more and more of the school-age population were nonwhite, Hispanic, and immigrant children from Latin America and Asia. With the realization that schools could not alter the structure of social and economic inequality came a reluctance to make equity the focus of education.

Federal involvement in education also had ambiguous consequences. Federal initiatives in compensatory education, educational rights for the handicapped and bilingualism, the National Institute of Education and a new Department of Education, evaluations and assessments of educational policies and practices like the Coleman Report and the National Assessment of Educational Progress, and court decisions on racial desegregation, affirmative action, school finance, student rights, and the outcomes of schooling all pressed local educational agencies to engage in efforts to enhance equity in education. But those policies provoked controversy and conflict. Expectations that there could be a consensus on what schools ought to do fragmented. Although federal funds usually amounted to less than 10 percent of a school district's budget and federal officials were rarely as omnipresent as critics suggested, federal requirements aroused indignation, their results were inconsistent, and they were costly to implement. By the late 1970s, sufficient criticism of federal intervention had mounted so that federal activism was on the retreat. The federal government was the most important protector of educational equity and educational opportunity, but there was widespread disenchantment with federal intervention (Harvard Educational Review, 1982).

There was a third ambiguity, over whether the schools had changed very much. To some, the changes had been dramatic, but whether they were advantageous was uncertain. While some argued that the new populations in school were being taught in more effective ways, others condemned declining academic standards and chaos in the curriculum. Yet, the continuities were substantial. Most teachers taught in much the same ways they had for decades. Many of the criticisms of low standards and poor teaching mirrored earlier criticisms. The dominance of peer-group relationships and the extracurriculum in the high schools and colleges was little different than for earlier generations. The vocationalization of schooling so apparent in the 1970s had been central to educational purposes for decades. The 1960s and 1970s had witnessed extraordinary ferment, but it was unclear just how different American education had become.

PART 5: DILEMMAS OF THE 1980s

The 1980s began with withering criticism of the schools and, quickly, the colleges for being academically sterile, of teachers for being inadequate to their tasks, of professors for being unconcerned with teaching, of federal intrusions, and of misguided idealism. The condemnations suggested how uncertain Americans felt about their schools.

Two widely publicized reports revealed the emotional intensity of the relationships between equality and excellence that had become the central dilemma of American education. The first, the report of the President's National Commission on Excellence in Education, *A Nation at Risk* (1983), began by condemning the academic and moral decline of the schools, what it called "a rising tide of mediocrity that threatens our very future as a Nation and a people." To the commission, the events of the previous decades seemed almost unremitting evidence of failure; in the quest to make equity and equality of opportunity the central purpose of schooling, Americans had destroyed excellence. In the commission's view, the primary aim of the 1980s was to redress the balance. [Document 33]

The second report, *Barriers to Excellence: Our Children at Risk* (1985), by the National Coalition of Advocates for Students, reasserted the view that equality of educational opportunity ought to be a fundamental ideal of the schools. It suggested that despite the efforts of the previous decades, minority, handicapped, and non-English-speaking children were still being treated as second-class citizens within the educational system. Rather than viewing the equity reforms as failures, it pointed out that compensatory education programs and Head Start had improved school achievement for those who participated in them and that rather than curb those programs, they and others like them should be expanded. The lessons of the past thus suggested greater federal efforts in support of educational opportunity, not less. [Document 34]

The two reports were part of a larger chorus of voices that once again put educational issues on the national agenda. Vigorous debate occurred over moral values, over aid to religious schools, over ways of bringing business into alliance with the schools, and over computers in education. While many of the voices were at the national level, more of them were working in the states. Governors articulated new commitments to education. State legislatures mandated more stringent graduation requirements and state-wide learning assessments. Higher salaries, merit pay, and career ladders were proposed to increase the attractiveness of teaching, while more rigorous certification measures were suggested to improve teacher competence. School districts developed programs to increase academic standards and revised their curricula. Teachers' organizations called for improved working conditions. A wave of reform efforts directed at the colleges and universities emerged, demanding that greater attention be paid to a "core" of knowledge and skills that undergraduates ought to possess and that graduate professional programs be strengthened.

If Americans needed help in understanding just how central schools had become to American life, the debates of the 1980s were an instant reminder. During the course of the twentieth century, schooling had become dramatically more prominent in the lives of countless Americans. Few individuals were untouched by it. Educational opportunity had become a measure of the aspirations and possibilities of American democracy. Educational failures—to provide access to education, to eliminate illiteracy, to extend intellectual and cultural horizons, and to free education from discrimination based on race, class, and gender—attested to the limitations of that democracy. The association, so ably noted by John Dewey in *Democracy and Education* (1916), between a democratic society and education had become a fundamental tenet of American society. Democracy and education were inextricably linked, and because of that schools would remain the most critical—and the most criticized—public institution.

REFERENCES

Aiken, Wilford M. *The Story of the Eight-Year Study*. New York: Harper & Brothers, 1942.

American Historical Association. *A Charter for the Social Sciences in the Schools*. New York: Charles Scribner's Sons, 1932.

Antler, Joyce. *Lucy Sprague Mitchell: A Biography*. New Haven: Yale University Press, 1986.

Bell, Howard M. *Youth Tell Their Story*. Washington, D.C.: American Council on Education, 1938.

Bledstein, Burton J. *The Culture of Professionalism: The Middle Class and the Development of Higher Education in America*. New York: W. W. Norton, 1976.

Chafe, William H. *Civilities and Civil Rights: Greensboro, North Carolina, and the Black Struggle for Freedom*. New York: Oxford University Press, 1980.

Cohen, David K. "Origins." In *The Shopping Mall High School: Winners and Losers in the Educational Marketplace*, by Arthur Powell, Eleanor Farrar, and David K. Cohen. Boston: Houghton Mifflin, 1985.

Counts, George S. *Dare the School Build a New Social Order?* New York: John Day, 1932.

Cremin, Lawrence A. *The Transformation of the School: Progressivism in American Education, 1876-1957*. New York: Knopf, 1961.

Cuban, Larry. *How Teachers Taught: Constancy and Change in American Classrooms, 1890-1980*. New York: Longman, 1984.

Cuban, Larry. *Teachers and Machines: The Classroom Use of Technology Since 1920*. New York: Teachers College Press, 1986.

Dewey, John. *Democracy and Education*. New York: MacMillian, 1916.

DuBois, W. E. B. *The Souls of the Black Folk*. New York: NAL, 1969; orig. pub. 1903.

Fass, Paula S. *The Damned and the Beautiful: American Youth in the 1920s*. New York: Oxford University Press, 1977.

Fass, Paula S. "Without Design: Education Policy in the New Deal." *American Journal of Education* 91 (Nov.1982): 36-64.

Featherstone, Joseph. *Schools Where Children Learn*. New York: Liveright, 1971.

FitzGerald, Frances. *America Revised: History Textbooks in the Twentieth Century*. Boston: Little, Brown, 1979.

Franklin, Barry M. *Building the American Community: The School Curriculum and the Search for Social Control*. Philadelphia: The Falmer Press, 1986.

Franklin, Vincent P. *The Education of Black Philadelphia: The Social*

and Educational History of a Minority Community, 1900–1950.
Philadelphia: University of Pennsylvania Press, 1979.

Geiger, Roger L. *To Advance Knowledge: The Growth of American
Research Universities, 1900–1940*. New York: Oxford University
Press, 1986.

Grubb, W. Norton, and Lazerson, Marvin. "Child Care, Government
Financing, and the Public Schools: Lessons from the California
Children's Centers." *School Review* 86 (Nov. 1977).

Haley, Margaret A. *Battleground: The Autobiography of Margaret A.
Haley*. Urbana: University of Illinois Press, 1982.

Hampel, Robert. *The Last Little Citadel: American High Schools Since
1940*. Boston: Houghton Mifflin, 1986.

Harlan, Lewis R. *Booker T. Washington: The Wizard of Tuskegee,
1901–1915*. New York: Oxford University Press, 1983.

Harlan, Lewis R. *Booker T. Washington: The Making of a Black Leader, 1856–1901*. New York: Oxford University Press, 1972.

Harvard Educational Review. *Rethinking the Federal Role in Education*
52 (Nov. 1982).

Harvard University. *General Education in a Free Society*. Cambridge:
Harvard University Press, 1945.

Hogan, David J. *Class and Reform: School and Society in Chicago,
1880–1930*. Philadelphia: University of Pennsylvania Press, 1985.

Homel, Michael W. *Down from Equality: Black Chicagoans and the
Public Schools, 1920–41*. Urbana: University of Illinois Press,
1984.

Horowitz, Helen Lefkowitz. *Alma Mater: Design and Experience in the
Women's Colleges from Their Nineteenth-Century Beginnings to
the 1930s*. New York: Knopf, 1984.

James, Thomas. "Life Begins with Freedom: The College Nisei, 1942–
1945." *History of Education Quarterly* 25 (Spring–Summer, 1985).

Jeffrey, Julie Roy. *Education for Children of the Poor: A Study of the
Origins and Implementation of the Elementary and Secondary Education Act of 1965*. Columbus: Ohio State University Press, 1978.

Jencks, Christopher; Smith, Marshall; Acland, Henry; Bane, Mary Jo;
Cohen, David; Gintis, Herbert; Heyns, Barbara; and Michelson,
Stephan. *Inequality: A Reassessment of the Effect of Family and
Schooling in America*. New York: Basic Books, 1972.

Kaestle, Carl F. *Pillars of the Republic: Common Schools and American Society, 1780–1860*. New York: Hill & Wang, 1983.

Kantor, Harvey. *"Learning to Earn": The Origins of Vocational Education in California, 1900-1930*. Madison: University of Wisconsin Press, 1987.

Kantor, Harvey, and Tyack, David. *Work, Youth, and Schooling: Historical Perspectives on Vocationalism in American Education*. Stanford: Stanford University Press, 1982.

Katznelson, Ira, and Weir, Margaret. *Schooling for All: Class, Race, and the Decline of the Democratic Ideal*. New York: Basic Books, 1985.

Kett, Joseph F. *Rites of Passage: Adolescence in America, 1790 to the Present*. New York: Basic Books, 1977.

Kliebard, Herbert. *The Struggle for the American Curriculum, 1893-1958*. Boston: Routledge and Kegan Paul, 1986.

Kluger, Richard. *Simple Justice: The History of Brown v. Board of Education and Black America's Struggle for Equality*. New York: Knopf, 1976.

Kohl, Herbert. *36 Children*. New York: NAL, 1967.

Kozol, Jonathan. *Death at an Early Age*. Boston: Houghton Mifflin, 1967.

Krug, Edward. *The Shaping of the American High School*. Madison: University of Wisconsin Press, 1964, 1972.

Lagemann, Ellen Condliffe. *Private Power for the Public Good: A History of the Carnegie Foundation for the Advancement of Teaching*. Middletown, Conn.: Wesleyan University Press, 1983.

Lazerson, Marvin. *Origins of the Urban School: Public Education in Massachusetts, 1870-1915*. Cambridge: Harvard University Press, 1971.

Lazerson, Marvin, and Grubb, W. Norton. *American Education and Vocationalism: Documents in the History of Vocational Education, 1870-1970*. New York: Teachers College Press, 1974.

Lazerson, Marvin; McLaughlin, Judith Block; McPherson, Bruce; and Bailey, Stephen K. *An Education of Value: The Purposes and Practices of American Schools*. New York: Cambridge University Press, 1985.

Levine, Daniel O. *The American College and the Culture of Aspiration, 1915-1940*. Ithaca: Cornell University Press, 1986.

Lukas, J. Anthony. *Common Ground: A Turbulent Decade in the Lives of Three American Families*. New York: Knopf, 1985.

Lynd, Robert, and Lynd, Helen Merrell. *Middletown: A Study in Mod-

ern American Culture. New York: Harcourt Brace, 1929.

Lynd, Robert, and Lynd, Helen Merrell. *Middletown in Transition: A Study in Cultural Conflict*. New York: Harcourt Brace, 1937.

Mirel, Jeffrey. "The Politics of Educational Retrenchment in Detroit, 1929-1935." *History of Education Quarterly* 24 (Fall 1984): 323-358.

Monti, Daniel J. *A Semblance of Justice: St. Louis School Desegregation and Order in Urban America*. Columbia: University of Missouri Press, 1985.

Nasaw, David. *Schooled to Order: A Social History of Public Schooling in the U.S.* New York: Oxford University Press, 1979.

Oleson, Alexandra, and Voss, John, eds. *The Organization of Knowledge in Modern America, 1860-1920*. Baltimore: Johns Hopkins Press, 1979.

Olneck, Michael, and Lazerson, Marvin. "Ethnicity and Education." In *Harvard University Encyclopedia of Ethnic Groups in American Life*, edited by Stephan Thernstrom. Cambridge: Harvard University Press, 1980.

Olsen, Keith W. *The G.I. Bill, the Veterans, and the Colleges*. Lexington: University Press of Kentucky, 1974.

Peterson, Paul E. *The Politics of School Reform, 1870-1940*. Chicago: University of Chicago Press, 1985.

Ravitch, Diane. *The Troubled Crusade: American Education, 1945-1980*. New York: Basic Books, 1983.

Reese, William J. *Power and the Promise of School Reform: Grassroots Movements During the Progressive Era*. Boston: Routledge and Kegan Paul, 1986.

Rudoph, Fredrick E. *Curriculum*. San Francisco: Jossey-Bass, 1977.

Silberman, Charles. *Crisis in the Classroom: The Remaking of American Education*. New York: Random House, 1970.

Solomon, Barbara Miller. *In the Company of Educated Women: A History of Women in Higher Education in America*. New York: Yale University Press, 1985.

Spring, Joel. *The American School, 1642-1985*. New York: Longman, 1986.

Spring, Joel. *The Sorting Machine: National Educational Policy Since 1945*. New York: David McKay, 1976.

Synott, Marcia G. *The Half-Opened Door: Discrimination and Admission at Harvard, Yale, and Princeton, 1900-1970*. Westport, Conn.: Greenwood Press, 1979.

Tyack, David. *The One-Best System: A History of American Urban Education*. Cambridge: Harvard University Press, 1974.

Tyack, David, and Hansot, Elizabeth. *Managers of Virtue: Public School Leadership in America, 1820–1980*. New York: Basic Books, 1982.

Tyack, David; Lowe, Robert; and Hansot, Elizabeth. *Public Schools in Hard Times: The Great Depression and Recent Years*. Cambridge: Harvard University Press, 1984.

U.S. Commission on Civil Rights. *Racial Isolation in the Public Schools*. Washington, D.C.: U.S. Government Printing Office, 1967.

Urban, Wayne J. *Why Teachers Organized*. Detroit: Wayne State University Press, 1982.

Veysey, Laurence R. *The Emergence of the American University*. Chicago: University of Chicago Press, 1965.

Waller, Willard W. *The Sociology of Teaching*. New York: John Wiley & Sons, 1967; orig. pub. 1932.

Wrigley, Julia. *Class Politics and Public Schools: Chicago, 1900–1950*. New Brunswick: Rutgers University Press, 1982.

1

The Transformation of Education 1900–1929

1. Industrial Education for the Negro (1903)

At the turn of the century, Booker T. Washington was America's most prominent spokesperson for black education. As head of Tuskegee Institute in Alabama, he articulated the value of an education in hard work and thrift and in occupationally useful skills, arguing that these were essential to economic success. His policies had broad implications for education, beyond its aims for black Americans.

In what I say here I would not by any means have it understood that I would limit or circumscribe the mental development of the Negro student. No race can be lifted until its mind is awakened and strengthened. By the side of industrial training should always go mental and moral training, but the pushing of mere abstract knowledge into the head means little. We want more than the mere performance of mental gymnastics. Our knowledge must be harnessed to the things of real life. I would encourage the Negro to secure all the mental strength, all the mental culture — whether gleaned from science, mathematics, history, language or literature that his circumstances will allow, but I believe most earnestly that for years to come the education of the people of my race should be so directed that the greatest proportion of the mental

SOURCE: Booker T. Washington, "Industrial Education for the Negro," in B. T. Washington et al., *The Negro Problem: A Series of Articles by Representative American Negroes of Today* (New York: J. Pott & Co., 1903; republished by Arno Press, 1969), pp. 16–23, 28–29.

strength of the masses will be brought to bear upon the every-day practical things of life, upon something that is needed to be done, and something which they will be permitted to do in the community in which they reside. . . .

I would teach the race that in industry the foundation must be laid—that the very best service which any one can render to what is called the higher education is to teach the present generation to provide a material or industrial foundation. On such a foundation as this will grow habits of thrift, a love of economy, ownership of property, bank accounts. Out of it in the future will grow practical education, professional education, positions of public responsibility. Out of it will grow moral and religious strength. Out of it will grow wealth from which alone can come leisure and the opportunity for the enjoyment of literature and the fine arts. . . .

I would set no limits to the attainments of the Negro in arts, in letters or statesmanship, but I believe the surest way to reach those ends is by laying the foundation in the little things of life that lie immediately about one's door. I plead for industrial education and development for the Negro not because I want to cramp him, but because I want to free him. I want to see him enter the all-powerful business and commercial world. . . .

Early in the history of the Tuskegee Institute we began to combine industrial training with mental and moral culture. Our first efforts were in the direction of agriculture, and we began teaching this with no appliances except one hoe and a blind mule. From this small beginning we have grown until now the Institute owns two thousand acres of land, eight hundred of which are cultivated each year by the young men of the school. We began teaching wheelwrighting and blacksmithing in a small way to the men, and laundry work, cooking and sewing and housekeeping to the young women. The fourteen hundred and over young men and women who attended the school during the last school year received instruction — in addition to academic and religious training — in thirty-three trades and industries, including carpentry, blacksmithing, printing, wheelwrighting, harnessmaking, painting, machinery, founding, shoemaking, brickmasonry and brickmaking, plastering, sawmilling, tinsmithing, tailoring, mechanical and architectural drawing, electrical and steam engineering, canning, sewing, dressmaking, millinery, cooking, laundering, housekeeping, mattress making, basketry, nursing, agriculture, dairying and stock raising, horticulture.

Not only do the students receive instruction in these trades, but they do actual work, by means of which more than half of them pay some part or all of their expenses while remaining at the school. Of the sixty buildings belonging to the school all but four were almost wholly erected by the students as a part of their industrial education. Even the bricks which go into the walls are made by students in the school's brick yard, in which, last year, they manufactured two million bricks. . . .

I close, then, as I began, by saying that as a slave the Negro was worked, and that as a freeman he must learn to work. There is still doubt in many quarters as to the ability of the Negro unguided, unsupported, to hew his own path and put into visible, tangible, indisputable form, products and signs of civilization. This doubt cannot be much affected by abstract arguments, no matter how delicately and convincingly woven together. Patiently, quietly, doggedly, persistently, through summer and

winter, sunshine and shadow, by self-sacrifice, by fore-
sight, by honesty and industry, we must re-enforce argument with results. One farm bought, one house built, one
home sweetly and intelligently kept, one man who is the
largest tax payer or has the largest bank account, one
school or church maintained, one factory running suc-
cessfully, one truck garden profitably cultivated, one patient cured by a Negro doctor, one sermon well preached,
one office well filled, one life cleanly lived — these will tell
more in our favor than all the abstract eloquence that can
be summoned to plead our cause. Our pathway must be
up through the soil, up through swamps, up through for-
ests, up through the streams, the rocks, up through commerce, education and religion!

2. The Talented Tenth (1903)

*W. E. B. DuBois's claim for the importance of a "Talented
Tenth" to lead black Americans into full participation in
American life led him to focus attention on higher education. Often in conflict with Booker T. Washington, he
nonetheless shared with Washington the view that education was crucial to the future of black Americans.*

The Negro race, like all races, is going to be saved by its
exceptional men. The problem of education, then, among
Negroes must first of all deal with the Talented Tenth; it is

SOURCE: W. E. B. DuBois, "The Talented Tenth," in B. T. Washington et al., *The Negro Problem: A Series of Articles by Representative
American Negroes of Today* (New York: J. Pott & Co., 1903; republished by Arno Press, 1969), pp. 33–35, 45–46, 56–60, 74–75.

the problem of developing the Best of this race that they may guide the Mass away from the contamination and death of the Worst, in their own and other races. Now the training of men is a difficult and intricate task. Its technique is a matter for educational experts, but its object is for the vision of seers. If we make money the object of man-training, we shall develop money-makers but not necessarily men; if we make technical skill the object of education, we may possess artisans but not, in nature, men. Men we shall have only as we make manhood the object of the work of the schools—intelligence, broad sympathy, knowledge of the world that was and is, and of the relation of men to it—this is the curriculum of that Higher Education which must underlie true life. On this foundation we may build bread winning, skill of hand and quickness of brain, with never a fear lest the child and man mistake the means of living for the object of life. . . .

How then shall the leaders of a struggling people be trained and the hands of the risen few strengthened? There can be but one answer: The best and most capable of their youth must be schooled in the colleges and universities of the land. We will not quarrel as to just what the university of the Negro should teach or how it should teach it—I willingly admit that each soul and each race-soul needs its own peculiar curriculum. But this is true: A university is a human invention for the transmission of knowledge and culture from generation to generation, through the training of quick minds and pure hearts, and for this work no other human invention will suffice, not even trade and industrial schools. . . .

The main question, so far as the Southern Negro is concerned, is: What under the present circumstances, must a system of education do in order to raise the Negro as quickly as possible in the scale of civilization? The answer to this question seems to me clear: It must strengthen the Negro's character, increase his knowledge and teach him to earn a living. Now it goes without saying, that it is hard to do all these things simultaneously or suddenly, and that at the same time it will not do to give all the attention to one and neglect the others; we could give black boys trades, but that alone will not civilize a race of ex-slaves; we might simply increase their knowledge of the world, but this would not necessarily make them wish to use this knowledge honestly; we might seek to strengthen character and purpose, but to what end if these people have nothing to eat or wear? A system of education is not one thing, nor does it have a single definite object, nor is it a mere matter of schools. Education is that whole system of human training within and without the school house walls, which molds and develops men. If then we start out to train an ignorant and unskilled people with a heritage of bad habits, our system of training must set before itself two great aims—the one dealing with knowledge and character, the other part seeking to give the child the technical knowledge necessary for him to earn a living under the present circumstances. These objects are accomplished in part by the opening of the common schools on the one, and of the industrial schools on the other. But only in part, for there must also be trained those who are to teach in these schools—men and women of knowledge and culture and technical skill who understand modern civilization, and have the training and aptitude to impart it to the children under them. There must be teachers, and teachers of teachers, and to attempt to establish any sort of system of common and industrial school training, without first (and I say first advisedly) without first providing for the higher training of the very best teachers, is simply throwing your money to the winds. School houses do not teach themselves — piles of brick and mortar and machinery do not send out men. . . .

I am an earnest advocate of manual training and trade teaching for black boys, and for white boys, too. I believe that next to the founding of Negro colleges the most valuable addition to Negro education since the war, has been industrial training for black boys. Nevertheless, I insist that the object of all true education is not to make men carpenters, it is to make carpenters men; there are two means of making the carpenter a man, each equally important: the first is to give the group and community in which he works, liberally trained teachers and leaders to teach him and his family what life means; the second is to give him sufficient intelligence and technical skill to make him an efficient workman; the first object demands the Negro college and college-bred men — not a quantity of such colleges, but a few of excellent quality; not too many college-bred men, but enough to leaven the lump, to inspire the masses, to raise the Talented Tenth to leadership; the second object demands a good system of common schools, well-taught, conveniently located and properly equipped. . . .

Men of America, the problem is plain before you. Here is a race transplanted through the criminal foolishness of your fathers. Whether you like it or not the millions are here, and here they will remain. If you do not lift them up, they will pull you down. Education and work are the levers to uplift a people. Work alone will not do it unless inspired by the right ideals and guided by intelligence.

Education must not simply teach work—it must teach Life. The Talented Tenth of the Negro race must be made leaders of thought and missionaries of culture among their people. No others can do this work and Negro colleges must train men for it. The Negro race, like all other races, is going to be saved by its exceptional men.

3. Why Teachers Should Organize (1904)

The charismatic leader of the Chicago Teachers Union Margaret Haley urged teachers to affiliate with organized labor and to think of themselves as professionals whose expertise entitled them to be the principle decision-makers in teaching and curriculum. Haley actively campaigned for tax reform, women's rights, and other progressive causes.

There is no possible conflict between the interest of the child and the interest of the teacher, and nothing so tends to make this fact evident as the progress in the scientific conception of educational method and administration. For both the child and the teacher freedom is the condition of development. The atmosphere in which it is easiest to teach is the atmosphere in which it is easiest to learn. The same things that are a burden to the teacher are a burden also to the child. The same things which restrict her powers restrict his powers also. . . .

Nowhere in the United States today does the public

SOURCE: Margaret A. Haley, "Why Teachers Should Organize," in National Education Association, *Proceedings* (1904), pp. 146, 148–151.

school, as a branch of the public service, receive from the public either the moral or financial support needed to enable it properly to perform its important function in the social organism. The conditions which are militating most strongly against efficient teaching, and which existing organizations of the kind under discussion here are directing their energies toward changing, briefly stated are the following:

1. Greatly increased cost of living, together with constant demands for higher standards of scholarship and professional attainments and culture, to be met with practically stationary and wholly inadequate teachers' salaries.

2. Insecurity of tenure of office and lack of provision for old age.

3. Overwork in the overcrowded schoolrooms, exhausting both mind and body.

4. And, lastly, lack of recognition of the teacher as an educator in the school system, due to the increased tendency toward "factoryizing education," making the teacher an automaton, a mere factory hand, whose duty it is to carry out mechanically and unquestioningly the ideas and orders of those clothed with the authority of position, and who may or may not know the needs of the children or how to minister to them.

The individuality of the teacher and her power of initiative are thus destroyed, and the result is courses of study, regulations, and equipment which the teachers have had no voice in selecting, which often have no relation to the children's needs, and which prove a hindrance instead of a help in teaching. . . .

In reacting unfavorably upon the public school, these wrong conditions affect the child, the parent, and the teacher; but the teacher is so placed that she is the one first to feel the disadvantage: she is held responsible by the child, by the parent, by the authorities, by society, and by herself because of her own ideals, for duties in the performance of which she is continually hampered. The dissatisfaction and restlessness among teachers are due to the growing consciousness that causes outside of themselves and beyond their control are making their work more difficult. . . .

The first and crudest form of expression that dissatisfaction with these conditions takes is the reaction against the nearest and most obvious cause of irritation — unsatisfactory supervision and administration, which are later recognized as effects rather than causes. The last causes to be assigned are the real ones, and only when every individual effort to better conditions has failed does the thought of combined effort for mutual aid — in other words, organized effort — suggest itself. . . .

Such organization is at once the effect and the cause of a broadening of the intelligence and the educational outlook of the teachers, for to such organization they must take not only a reading acquaintance with the best in educational theory and practice, but a practical knowledge of what constitutes scientific teaching. Nor is this all, tho it may suffice for the professional equipment of those whose duties are merely supervisory. The classroom teachers in addition to this must have the ability and skill, given fair conditions, to do scientific teaching. More than this, they must know the conditions under which scientific teaching is possible, must know when and in what respects such conditions are lacking; and then, most difficult of all, because it includes all these and much more, they must know how to reach the public with accurate information concerning the conditions under which teaching is done and their effects on the work of the school.

4. The Dewey School (1896–1903)

John Dewey's ideas found expression in the Laboratory School of the University of Chicago. In this excerpt, two teachers describe how they put Dewey's educational philosophy into curricular form.

The Laboratory School was both a department of the University and a place where parents sent children to be educated. As such it required conditions which would insure freedom for investigation on the one hand, and normal development for child life on the other. This meant the planning of a curriculum which was not static in character, but one which ministered constantly to the changing needs and interests of the growing child's experience. It involved careful arrangement of the physical and social set-up of the school and a discriminating search for subject-matter which would fulfill and further the growth of the whole child. . . .

A common center was found for the Laboratory School in the idea of the school-house as a home in which the activities of social or community life were carried on. The ideal was so to use and guide the child's interest in his

SOURCE: Katherine Camp Mayhew and Anna Camp Edwards, *The Dewey School: The Laboratory School of the University of Chicago, 1896–1903* (New York: Atherton, 1966; original 1936), pp. 20, 42–44. Reprinted by Permission of the publishers, Lieber-Atherton, Inc., Copyright © 1966. All rights reserved.

home, his natural environment, and in himself that he should gain social and scientifically sound notions of the functions of persons in the home; of plant and animal, including human life, and their interdependence; of the sun as the source of all energy; of heat as a special form of energy used in the home (as in cooking); and of food as stored energy. The materials about him and the things that were being done to and with them furnished the ideas for the initial start and choice of the activities which occupied the children in the shop, laboratory, kitchen, and studios. These ideas were chosen for study not alone because of their direct, clear, and explicit relationship to the child's own present environment and experience, but also because of their indirect, veiled, and implied relationship to the past out of which present conditions have developed and to the future which is dependent upon the present. They started the child in his present, interested him to relive the past, and in due time carried him on to future possibilities and achievements in an ever developing experience. In brief, they furnished a thread of continuity because they were concerned with the fundamental requisites of living.

From the teacher's standpoint, the development of these ideas afforded occasions and opportunities for the enrichment and extension of the child's experience in connection with his activities. The reconstructed story of the building of the homes of the primitive peoples, as the youngest group imagined and reenacted it, took on a character as real in historical quality as the authentic accounts of the homes of the ancient Greeks — the history learned by older groups. New words and short sentences, both read and written, added themselves easily to the vocabularies of the youngest children, while literature embodying beauty of the written work was given to them in myth and story that had to do with the activities they were carrying on. From the teacher's point of view, the child was learning art as he drew, daubed, or modeled the idea that urged him to expression. He, however, unconscious that he was learning anything, expressed in line or color, clay, wood, or softer fabric, the thing that in him lay and in so doing, no matter how crude the result, tasted of those deep satisfactions that attend all creative effort. Little did the experimenting child realize that he was studying physics as he boiled down his cane or maple syrup, watched the crystallization process, the effects of heat on water, and of both on the various grains used for food. He reinvented Ab's trap for the sabre-toothed tiger, quite oblivious that he was rediscovering the use of a certain kind of lever. The teacher knew, although he did not, that he was studying the chemistry of combustion as he figured out why fire burned, or weighed, burned, and weighed again the ashes from the different woods or coal and compared results. The coal in the bins in the cellar was traced to the mines and the fossil plants. The coal beds were located as were all the products used in the activities. From the teacher's standpoint, this was geology and geography, or biology as the children examined the seeds, their distribution, and use as food, or the life of the birds and animals in the open fields. From the child's standpoint, however, these ideas were interesting facts or skills that he learned as he went about his various occupations; they were reflected, as it were, in the series of activities through which he passed in becoming conscious of the basis of social life.

5. The University Ideal (1904)

The "Wisconsin Idea," as articulated by the incoming president of the University of Wisconsin, urged higher education to extend its responsibilities in American society. The model of expert service, research, and an array of curricular offerings quickly became the dominant ethos of twentieth-century American universities.

If time permitted, I should be glad to consider the effect of university work upon the mind of the student, that is, work in which he takes a share as an investigator and during which he acquires the spirit of research. It would be easy to show that the qualities of mind gained by such work are those which best fit him for the struggle of life—which best fit him to handle difficult business, social and economic problems. In Germany the university scholar is a man of affairs. He is found in all important divisions of administration. Almost every prominent German and Austrian professor is an official adviser to the government. Already, in America, we see the beginning of this movement. University professors are asked to serve on tax commissions, in the valuation of railroads and in other various capacities. Within the next half century the number of such men in these and similar positions will increase many fold. The college-trained man,

SOURCE: Charles R. Van Hise, "Inaugural Address," *Science* 20 (1904): 193–205. Copyright 1904 by the American Academy for the Advancement of Science.

and especially the university-trained man, is, directly or indirectly, to control the destinies of the nation. . . .

I, therefore, hold that the state university, a university which is to serve the state, must see to it that scholarship and research of all kinds, whether or not a possible practical value can be pointed out, must be sustained. A privately endowed institution may select some part of knowledge and confine itself to it, but not so a state university. A university supported by the state for all its people, for all its sons and daughters, with their tastes and aptitudes as varied as mankind, can place no bounds upon the lines of its endeavor, else the state is the irreparable loser.

Be the choice of the sons and daughters of the state, language, literature, history, political economy, pure science, agriculture, engineering, architecture, sculpture, painting or music, they should find at the state university ample opportunity for the pursuit of the chosen subject, even until they become creators in it. Nothing short of such opportunity is just, for each has an equal right to find at the state university the advanced intellectual life adapted to his need. Any narrower view is indefensible. The university should extend its scope until the field is covered from agriculture to the fine arts. . . .

We are now able to suggest the ideal American university — one which has the best features of the English system with its dormitories, commons and union; one which includes the liberal and fine arts and the additions of science and applied science; and one which superimposes upon these an advanced school modeled upon the German universities, but with a broader scope. In such a university the student in the colleges of liberal and fine arts has opportunity to elect work in applied science, and thus broaden his education. He feels the inspiring influence of scholarship and research, and thus gains enthusiasm for the elementary work because it leads to the heights. The student in applied knowledge is not restricted to subjects which concern his future profession, but he has the opportunity to pursue the humanities and the fine arts, and thus liberalize his education. He, too, feels the stimulus of the graduate school, and, if one of the elect, may become an investigator and thus further ameliorate the lot of mankind by new applications of science to life. The student in the graduate school, primarily concerned with creative scholarship, may supplement a deficient basal training by work in the liberal arts and in the schools of applied knowledge. Thus the college of liberal arts, of applied knowledge and of creative scholarship interlock. Each is stronger and can do the work peculiar to itself better than if alone. This combination university is the American university of the future, and this the University of Wisconsin must become if it is to be the peer of the great universities of the nation.

6. The Liberal College (1912)

An ardent defender of liberal education, Alexander Meiklejohn in his inaugural address as president of Amherst College proclaimed education of the mind the central mission of the college. In an era of growing spe-

SOURCE: Alexander Meiklejohn, "What the Liberal College Is," *Amherst Graduates Quarterly* 11 (1912). Republished in Alexander Meiklejohn, *The Liberal College* (Boston: Marshall Jones, 1920).

cialization, professionalization, and university domi-
nance, he determinedly sought to keep a place for the
undergraduate liberal arts curriculum.

What do our teachers believe to be the aim of college
instruction? Wherever their opinions and convictions
find expression there is one contention which is always in
the foreground, namely, that to be liberal a college must
be essentially intellectual. It is a place, the teachers tell
us, in which a boy, forgetting all things else, may set forth
on the enterprise of learning. It is a time when a young
man may come to awareness of the thinking of his people, may perceive what knowledge is and has been and is
to be. Whatever light-hearted undergraduates may say,
whatever the opinions of solicitous parents, of ambitious
friends, of employers in search of workmen, of leaders in
church or state or business — whatever may be the beliefs
and desires and demands of outsiders — the teacher within
the college, knowing his mission as no one else can know
it, proclaims that mission to be the leading of his pupil
into the life intellectual. The college is primarily not a
place of the body, nor of the feelings, nor even of the will;
it is, first of all, a place of the mind. . . .

In a word, the liberal college does not pretend to give
all the kinds of teaching which a young man of college
age may profitably receive; it does not even claim to give
all the kinds of intellectual training which are worth giving. It is committed to intellectual training of the liberal
type, whatever that may mean, and to that mission it
must be faithful. One may safely say, then, on behalf of
our college teachers, that their instruction is intended to
be radically different from that given in the technical
school or even in the professional school. Both these in-

stitutions are practical in a sense in which the college, as
an intellectual institution, is not. . . .

In the conflict with the forces within the college our
teachers find themselves fighting essentially the same bat-
tle as against the foes without. In a hundred ways the
friends of the college, students, graduates, trustees and
even colleagues, seem to them so to misunderstand its
mission as to minimize or to falsify its intellectual ideals.
The college is a good place for making friends; it gives
excellent experience in getting on with men; it has exceptional advantages as an athletic club; it is a relatively safe
place for a boy when he first leaves home; on the whole it
may improve a student's manners; it gives acquaintance
with lofty ideas of character, preaches the doctrine of
social service, exalts the virtues and duties of citizenship.
All these conceptions seem to the teacher to hide or to
obscure the fact that the college is fundamentally a place
of the mind, a time for thinking, an opportunity for
knowing.

7. The Flexner Report on Medical Education (1910)

*Commissioned by the Carnegie Foundation for the Ad-
vancement of Teaching, the Flexner Report proposed that
standards for medical education be greatly improved*

SOURCE: Abraham Flexner, *Medical Education in the United States
and Canada* (New York: Carnegie Foundation for the Advancement of
Teaching, 1910), Bulletin #4, pp. x–xi. Excerpt from the "Introduction"
by Henry S. Pritchett. © The Carnegie Foundation for the Advancement of Teaching. Reprinted by permission.

through the elimination of many medical schools and the expansion of hospital-based clinical training. The report's larger significance lay in its urging of university responsibility for professional education. This introduction to the report by the Foundation's president summarizes the findings.

The striking and significant facts which are here brought out are of enormous consequence not only to the medical practitioner, but to every citizen of the United States and Canada; for it is a singular fact that the organization of medical education in this country has hitherto been such as not only to commercialize the process of education itself, but also to obscure in the minds of the public any discrimination between the well trained physician and the physician who has had no adequate training whatsoever. As a rule, Americans, when they avail themselves of the services of a physician, make only the slightest inquiry as to what his previous training and preparation have been. One of the problems of the future is to educate the public itself to appreciate the fact that very seldom, under existing conditions, does a patient receive the best aid which it is possible to give him in the present state of medicine, and that this is due mainly to the fact that a vast army of men is admitted to the practice of medicine who are untrained in sciences fundamental to the profession and quite without a sufficient experience with disease. A right education of public opinion is one of the problems of future medical education.

The significant facts revealed by this study are these:

(1) For twenty-five years past there has been an enormous over-production of uneducated and ill trained medical practitioners. This has been in absolute disregard of

the public welfare and without any serious thought of the interests of the public. Taking the United States as a whole, physicians are four or five times as numerous in proportion to population as in older countries like Germany.

(2) Over-production of ill trained men is due in the main to the existence of a very large number of commercial schools, sustained in many cases by advertising methods through which a mass of unprepared youth is drawn out of industrial occupations into the study of medicine.

(3) Until recently the conduct of a medical school was a profitable business, for the methods of instruction were mainly didactic. As the need for laboratories has become more keenly felt, the expenses of an efficient medical school have been greatly increased. The inadequacy of many of these schools may be judged from the fact that nearly half of all our medical schools have incomes below $10,000, and these incomes determine the quality of instruction that they can and do offer.

Colleges and universities have in large measure failed in the past twenty-five years to appreciate the great advance in medical education and the increased cost of teaching it along modern lines. Many universities desirous of apparent educational completeness have annexed medical schools without making themselves responsible either for the standards of the professional schools or for their support.

(4) The existence of many of these unnecessary and inadequate medical schools has been defended by the argument that a poor medical school is justified in the interest of the poor boy. It is clear that the poor boy has no right to go into any profession for which he is not willing to obtain adequate preparation; but the facts set

forth in this report make it evident that this argument is insincere, and that the excuse which has hitherto been put forward in the name of the poor boy is in reality an argument in behalf of the poor medical school.

(5) A hospital under complete educational control is as necessary to a medical school as is a laboratory of chemistry or pathology. High grade teaching within a hospital introduces a most wholesome and beneficial influence into its routine. Trustees of hospitals, public and private, should therefore go to the limit of their authority in opening hospital wards to teaching, provided only that the universities secure sufficient funds on their side to employ as teachers men who are devoted to clinical science.

In view of these facts, progress for the future would seem to require a very much smaller number of medical schools, better equipped and better conducted than our schools now as a rule are; and the needs of the public would equally require that we have fewer physicians graduated each year, but that these should be better educated and better trained.

8. Cardinal Principles of Secondary Education (1918)

One of the most influential documents on secondary education in American history, the "Cardinal Principles" affirmed the practical utility of education. Its seven objec-

SOURCE: National Education Association, *Report of the Commission on the Reorganization of Secondary Education*, U.S. Bureau of Education Bulletin No. 35 (Washington, D.C.: Government Printing Office, 1918), pp. 7–16.

tives for the high school emphasized the importance of adapting education to social needs and required that the curriculum be especially concerned with immediate applicability. The report quickly became the organizing motif for future debates about secondary schooling.

Secondary education should be determined by the needs of the society to be served, the character of the individuals to be educated, and the knowledge of educational theory and practice available. These factors are by no means static. Society is always in process of development; the character of the secondary-school population undergoes modification; and the sciences on which educational theory and practice depend constantly furnish new information. Secondary education, however, like any other established agency of society, is conservative and tends to resist modification. Failure to make adjustments when the need arises leads to the necessity for extensive reorganization at irregular intervals. The evidence is strong that such a comprehensive reorganization of secondary education is imperative at the present time.

1. *Changes in society* — Within the past few decades changes have taken place in American life profoundly affecting the activities of the individual. As a citizen, he must to a greater extent and in a more direct way cope with problems of community life, State and National Governments, and international relationships. As a worker, he must adjust himself to a more complex economic order. As a relatively independent personality, he has more leisure. The problems arising from these three dominant phases of life are closely interrelated and call for a degree of intelligence and efficiency on the part of every citizen that can not be secured through elementary

education alone, or even through secondary education unless the scope of that education is broadened.

The responsibility of the secondary school is still further increased because many social agencies other than the school afford less stimulus for education than heretofore. In many vocations there have come such significant changes as the substitution of the factory system for the domestic system of industry; the use of machinery in place of manual labor; the high specialization of processes with a corresponding subdivision of labor; and the breakdown of the apprentice system. In connection with home and family life have frequently come lessened responsibility on the part of the children; the withdrawal of the father and sometimes the mother from home occupations to the factory or store; and increased urbanization, resulting in less unified family life. Similarly, many important changes have taken place in community life, in the church, in the State, and in other institutions. These changes in American life call for extensive modifications in secondary education.

2. Changes in the secondary-school population — In the past 25 years there have been marked changes in the secondary-school population of the United States. . . . The character of the secondary-school population has been modified by the entrance of large numbers of pupils of widely varying capacities, aptitudes, social heredity, and destinies in life. Further, the broadening of the scope of secondary education has brought to the school many pupils who do not complete the full course but leave at various stages of advancement. The needs of these pupils can not be neglected, nor can we expect in the near future that all pupils will be able to complete the secondary school as full-time students. . . .

3. *Changes in educational theory* — The sciences on which educational theory depends have within recent years made significant contributions. In particular, educational psychology emphasizes the following factors:

(a) *Individual differences in capacities and aptitudes among secondary-school pupils.* Already recognized to some extent, this factor merits fuller attention.

(b) *The reexamination and reinterpretation of subject values and the teaching methods with reference to "general discipline."* While the final verdict of modern psychology has not as yet been rendered, it is clear that former conceptions of "general values" must be thoroughly revised.

(c) *Importance of applying knowledge.* Subject values and teaching methods must be tested in terms of the laws of learning and the application of knowledge to the activities of life, rather than primarily in terms of the demands of any subject as a logically organized science.

(d) *Continuity in the development of children.* It has long been held that psychological changes at certain stages are so pronounced as to overshadow the continuity of development. On this basis secondary education has been sharply separated from elementary education. Modern psychology, however, goes to show that the development of the individual is in most respects a continuous process and that, therefore, any sudden or abrupt break between the elementary and the secondary school or between any two successive stages of education is undesirable.

The foregoing changes in society, in the character of the secondary-school population, and in educational theory, together with many other considerations, call for extensive modifications of secondary education. . . .

This commission, therefore, regards the following as the main objectives of education: 1. Health. 2. Command of fundamental processes. 3. Worthy home-membership. 4. Vocation. 5. Citizenship. 6. Worthy use of leisure. 7. Ethical character.

The naming of the above objectives is not intended to imply that the process of education can be divided into separated fields. This cannot be, since the pupil is indivisible. Nor is the analysis all-inclusive. Nevertheless, we believe that distinguishing and naming these objectives will aid in directing efforts; and we hold that they should constitute the principal aims in education. . . .

1. *Health*—Health needs cannot be neglected during the period of secondary education without serious danger to the individual and the race. The secondary school should therefore provide health instruction, inculcate health habits, organize an effective program of physical activities, regard health needs in planning work and play, and cooperate with home and community in safe-guarding and promoting health interests. . . .

2. *Command of fundamental processes*—Much of the energy of the elementary school is properly devoted to teaching certain fundamental processes, such as reading, writing, arithmetical computations, and the elements of oral and written expression. The facility that a child of 12 or 14 may acquire in the use of these tools is not sufficient for the needs of modern life. This is particularly true of the mother tongue. . . . Throughout the secondary school, instruction and practice must go hand in hand, but as indicated in the report of the committee on English, only

so much theory should be taught at any one time as will show results in practice.

3. *Worthy home-membership* — Worthy home-membership as an objective calls for the development of those qualities that make the individual a worthy member of a family, both contributing to and deriving benefit from that membership.

This objective applies to both boys and girls. The social studies should deal with the home as a fundamental social institution and clarify its relation to the wider interests outside. Literature should interpret and idealize the human elements that go to make the home. . . . In the education of every high-school girl, the household arts should have a prominent place because of their importance to the girl herself and to others whose welfare will be directly in her keeping. . . .

4. *Vocation* — Vocational education should equip the individual to secure a livelihood for himself and those dependent on him, to serve well through his vocation, to maintain the right relationships toward his fellow workers and society, and, as far as possible, to find in that vocation his own best development.

This ideal demands that the pupil explore his own capacities and aptitudes, and make a survey of the world's work, to the end that he may select his vocation wisely. Hence, an effective program of vocational guidance in the secondary school is essential.

The extent to which the secondary school should offer training for a specific vocation depends upon the vocation, the facilities that the school can acquire, and the opportunity that the pupil may have to obtain such training later. To obtain satisfactory results those proficient in that vocation should be employed as instructors and the actual conditions of the vocation should be utilized either within the high school or in cooperation with the home, farm, shop, or office. Much of the pupil's time will be required to produce such efficiency.

5. *Civic education should develop in the individual those qualities whereby he will act well his part as a member of neighborhood, town or city, State, and Nation, and give him a basis for understanding international problems.* . . .

While all subjects should contribute to good citizenship, the social studies — geography, history, civics, and economics — should have this as their dominant aim. Too frequently, however, does mere information, conventional in value and remote in its bearing, make up the content of the social studies. History should so treat the growth of institutions that their present value may be appreciated. Geography should show the interdependence of men while it shows their common dependence on nature. Civics should concern itself less with constitutional questions and remote governmental functions, and should direct attention to social agencies close at hand and to the informal activities of daily life that regard and seek the common good. Such agencies as child-welfare organizations and consumers' leagues afford specific opportunities for the expression of civic qualities by the older pupils. . . .

The comprehension of the ideals of American democracy and loyalty to them should be a prominent aim of civic education. The pupil would feel that he will be responsible, in cooperation with others, for keeping the Nation true to the best inherited conceptions of democracy, and he should also realize that democracy itself is an ideal to be wrought out by his own and succeeding generations. . . .

6. *Worthy use of leisure* — Education should equip the individual to secure from his leisure the re-creation of body, mind, and spirit, and the enrichment and enlargement of his personality.

This objective calls for the ability to utilize the common means of enjoyment, such as music, art, literature, drama, and social intercourse, together with the fostering in each individual of one or more avocational interests.

Heretofore the high school has given little conscious attention to this objective. It has so exclusively sought intellectual discipline that it has seldom treated literature, art, and music so as to evoke the right emotional response and produce positive enjoyment. Its presentation of science should aim, in part, to arouse a genuine appreciation of nature.

The school has failed also to organize and direct the social activities of young people as it should. One of the surest ways in which to prepare pupils worthily to utilize leisure in adult life is by guiding and directing their use of leisure in youth. The school should, therefore, see that adequate recreation is provided both within the school and by other proper agencies in the community. The school, however, has a unique opportunity in this field because it includes in its membership representatives from all classes of society and consequently is able through social relationships to establish bonds of friendship and common understanding that cannot be furnished by other agencies. Moreover, the school can so organize recreational activities that they will contribute simultaneously to other ends of education, as in the case of the school pageant or festival.

7. *Ethical character* — In a democratic society ethical character becomes paramount among objectives of the

secondary school. Among the means for developing ethical character may be mentioned the wise selection of content and methods of instruction in all subjects of study, the social contacts of pupils with one another and with their teachers, the opportunities afforded by the organization and administration of the school for the development on the part of pupils of the sense of personal responsibility and initiative, and, above all, the spirit of service and the principles of true democracy which should permeate the entire school — principal, teachers, and pupils.

9. Schools in Middletown (1929)

In their classic study of Muncie, Indiana, during the mid-1920s, sociologists Robert and Helen Lynd described life in and out of schools. Their discussion of Muncie's pride in its schools, the dominance of vocational purposes and athletic and social activities, and the low status of teachers was a dramatic portrait of the purposes and practices of American education.

The school, like the factory, is a thoroughly regimented world. Immovable seats in orderly rows fix the sphere of activity of each child. For all, from the timid six-year-old entering for the first time to the most assured high school

SOURCE: Robert S. Lynd and Helen Merrell Lynd, *Middletown: A Study in American Culture* (New York: Harcourt, Brace & Co., 1929), pp. 188, 194–198, 206, 209, 211, 218–220. © 1937 by Harcourt Brace Jovanovich, Inc.; renewed 1965 by Robert S. and Helen M. Lynd. Reprinted by permission of the publisher.

senior, the general routine is much the same. Bells divide
the day into periods. For the six-year-olds the periods are
short (fifteen to twenty-five minutes) and varied; in some
they leave their seats, play games, and act out make-
believe stories, although in "recitation periods" all movement is prohibited. As they grow older the taboo upon
physical activity becomes stricter, until by the third or
fourth year practically all movement is forbidden except
the marching from one set of seats to another between
periods, a brief interval of prescribed exercise daily, and
periods of manual training or home economics once or
twice a week. There are "study-periods" in which children
learn "lessons" from "textbooks" prescribed by the state
and "recitation-periods" in which they tell an adult teacher what the book has said; one hears children reciting the
battles of the Civil War in one recitation period, the rivers
of Africa in another, the "parts of speech" in a third; the
method is much the same. With high school come some
differences; more "vocational" and "laboratory" work
varies the periods. But here again the lesson-text-book-
recitation method is the chief characteristic of education.
For nearly an hour a teacher asks questions and pupils
answer, then a bell rings, on the instant books bang, pow-
der and mirrors come out, there is a buzz of talk and
laughter as all the urgent business of living resumes mo-
mentarily for the children, notes and "dates" are ex-
changed, five minutes pass, another bell, gradual sliding
into seats, a final giggle, a last vanity case snapped shut,
"in our last lesson we had just finished" – and another
class is begun. . . .

The most pronounced region of movement appears in
the rush of courses that depart from the traditional digni-
fied conception of what constitutes education and seek to

train for specific tool and skill activities in factory, office, and home. A generation ago a solitary optional senior course in bookkeeping was the thin entering wedge of the trend that today controls eight of the twelve courses [of study] of the high school and claimed 17 per cent of the total student hours during the first semester of 1923–24 and 21 per cent during the second. At no point has the training prescribed for the preparation of children for effective adulthood approached more nearly actual preparation for the dominant concerns in the daily lives of the people of Middletown. This pragmatic commandeering of education is frankly stated by the president of the School Board: "For a long time all boys were trained to be President. Then for a while we trained them all to be professional men. Now we are training boys to get jobs." . . .

Under the circumstances, it is not surprising that this vocational work for boys is the darling of Middletown's eye – if we except a group of teachers and of parents of the business class who protest that the city's preoccupation with vocational work tends to drag down standards in academic studies and to divert the future college student's attention from his preparatory courses. Like the enthusiastically supported high school basketball team, these vocational courses have caught the imagination of the mass of male tax-payers; ask your neighbor at Rotary what kind of schools Middletown has and he will begin to tell you about these "live" courses. It is not without significance that vocational supervisors are more highly paid than any other teachers in the school system.

Much of what has been said of the strictly vocational courses applies also to work in bookkeeping and stenography and in home economics. The last-named, entirely new since 1890, is devised to meet the functional needs of the major group of the girls, who will be home-makers. . . . As in the boys' vocational work, these courses center in the more obvious, accepted group practices; much more of the work in home economics, for example, centers in the traditional household productive skills such as canning, baking, and sewing, than in the rapidly growing battery of skills involved in effective buying of ready-made articles. . . .

Second only in importance to the rise of these courses addressed to practical and vocational activities is the new emphasis upon courses in history and civics. These represent yet another point at which Middletown is bending its schools to the immediate service of its institutions—in this case, bolstering community solidarity against sundry divisive tendencies. . . . The president of the Board of Education, addressing a meeting of Middletown parents in 1923, said that "many educators have failed to face the big problem of teaching patriotism. . . . We need to teach American children about American heroes and American ideals." . . .

In the school as in the home, child-training is largely left to the womenfolk. Four-fifths of Middletown's teachers are women, the majority of them unmarried women under forty. This is not the result of a definite policy, although the general sentiment of the community probably accords with at least the first half of the local editorial statement in 1900 that teaching is "an occupation for which women seem to have a peculiar fitness and a greater adaptability than men; but whether from their qualities of gentleness or from superior mental endowment is open to question." Actually, however, here as at so many other points in the city's life, money seems to be the controlling factor; more money elsewhere draws men away from teaching, rather than special fitness attracting women. Middletown pays its teachers more than it did thirty-five years ago, but even the $2,100 maximum paid to grade school principals and high school teachers, the $3,200 paid to the high school principal, and the $4,900 to the Superintendent of Schools are hardly enough to tempt many of the abler men away from business in a culture in which everything hinges on money. . . .

Few things about education in Middletown today are more noteworthy than the fact that the entire community treats its teachers casually. These more than 250 persons to whom this weighty responsibility of training the young is entrusted are not the wise, skilled, revered elders of the group. In terms of the concerns and activities that preoccupy the keenest interests of the city's leaders, they are for the most part nonentities; rarely does one run across a teacher at the weekly luncheons of the city's business men assembled in their civic clubs; nor are many of them likely to be present at social functions over which the wives of these influential men preside. Middletown pays these people to whom it entrusts its children about what it pays a retail clerk, turns the whole business of running the schools over to a School Board of three business men appointed by the political machine, and rarely stumbles on the individual teacher thereafter save when a particularly interested mother pays a visit to the school "to find out how Ted is getting along." The often bitter comments of the teachers themselves upon their lack of status and recognition in the ordinary give and take of local life are not needed to make an observer realize that in this commercial culture the "teacher" and "professor" do not occupy the position they did even a generation ago. . . .

Accompanying the formal training afforded by courses of study is another and informal kind of training, particularly during the high school years. The high school, with its athletics, clubs, sororities and fraternities, dances and parties, and other "extracurricular activities," is a fairly complete social cosmos in itself, and about this city within a city the social life of the intermediate generation centers. . . . This informal training is not a preparation for a vague future that must be taken on trust, as is the case with so much of the academic work; to many of the boys and girls in high school this is "the life," the thing they personally like best about going to school. . . .

The relative disregard of most people in Middletown for teachers and for the content of books, on the one hand, and the exalted position of the social and athletic activities of the schools, on the other, offer an interesting commentary on Middletown's attitude toward education. And yet Middletown places large faith in going to school. The heated opposition to compulsory education in the nineties has virtually disappeared; only three of the 124 working class families interviewed voiced even the mildest impatience at it. Parents insist upon more and more education as part of their children's birthright; editors and lecturers point to education as a solution for every kind of social ill; the local press proclaims, "Public Schools of [Middletown] Are the City's Pride"; woman's club papers speak of the home, the church, and the school as the "foundations" of Middletown's culture. Education is a faith, a religion, to Middletown. And yet when one looks more closely at this dominant belief in the magic of formal schooling, it appears that it is not what actually goes on in the schoolroom that these many voices laud. Literacy, yes, they want their children to be able to "read the newspapers, write a letter, and perform the ordinary operations of arithmetic," but, beyond that, many of them are little interested in what the schools teach. This thing, education, appears to be desired frequently not for its specific content but as a symbol — by the working class as an open sesame that will mysteriously admit their children to a world closed to them, and by the business class as a heavily sanctioned aid in getting on further economically or socially in the world.

2

Continuity and Change
1930–1941

10. Dare the School Build a New Social Order? (1932)

After a series of critiques on the social class bias of American education during the 1920s, George Counts of Teachers College, Columbia University, issued this stirring plea to educators to use the school in the task of social reconstruction. Counts found in the Depression of the 1930s the failure of individualism and capitalism and claimed that conditions were ripe for democratic collectivism.

Like all simple and unsophisticated peoples we Americans have a sublime faith in education. Faced with any difficult problem of life we set our minds at rest sooner or later by the appeal to the school. We are convinced that education is the one unfailing remedy for every ill to which man is subject, whether it be vice, crime, war, poverty, riches, injustice, racketeering, political corruption, race hatred, class conflict, or just plain original sin. We even speak glibly and often about the general reconstruction of society through the school. We cling to this faith in spite of the fact that the very period in which our troubles have multiplied so rapidly has witnessed an unprecedented expansion of organized education. This

SOURCE: George S. Counts, *Dare the School Build a New Social Order?* (New York: The John Day Co., 1932; republished by Arno Press, 1969), pp. 3–7, 9–10. © 1932 by George S. Counts. Reprinted by permission of Harper & Row, Publishers, Inc.

would seem to suggest that our schools, instead of directing the course of change, are themselves driven by the
very forces that are transforming the rest of the social
order.

The bare fact, however, that simple and unsophisticated peoples have unbounded faith in education does not
mean that the faith is untenable. History shows that the
intuitions of such folk may be nearer the truth than the
weighty and carefully reasoned judgments of the learned
and the wise. Under certain conditions education may be
as beneficent and as powerful as we are wont to think.
But if it is to be so, teachers must abandon much of their
easy optimism, subject the concept of education to the
most rigorous scrutiny, and be prepared to deal much
more fundamentally, realistically, and positively with the
American social situation than has been their habit in the
past. Any individual or group that would aspire to lead
society must be ready to pay the costs of leadership: to
accept responsibility, to suffer calumny, to surrender security, to risk both reputation and future. . . .

That the existing school is leading the way to a better
social order is a thesis which few informed persons would
care to defend. Except as it is forced to fight for its own
life during times of depression, its course is too serene
and untroubled. Only in the rarest of instances does it
wage war on behalf of principle or ideal. Almost every-
where it is in the grip of conservative forces and is serving
the cause of perpetuating ideas and institutions suited to
an age that is gone. But there is one movement above the
educational horizon which would seem to show promise
of genuine and creative leadership. I refer to the Progressive Education movement. Surely in this union of two of
the great faiths of the American people, the faith in
progress and the faith in education, we have reason to

hope for light and guidance. Here is a movement which would seem to be completely devoted to the promotion of social welfare through education.

Even a casual examination of the program and philosophy of the Progressive schools, however, raises many doubts in the mind. To be sure, these schools have a number of large achievements to their credit. They have focused attention squarely upon the child; they have recognized the fundamental importance of the interest of the learner; they have defended the thesis that activity lies at the root of all true education; they have conceived learning in terms of life situations and growth of character; they have championed the rights of the child as a free personality. Most of this is excellent, but in my judgment it is not enough. It constitutes too narrow a conception of the meaning of education; it brings into the picture but one-half of the landscape. . . .

The weakness of Progressive Education thus lies in the fact that it has elaborated no theory of social welfare, unless it be that of anarchy or extreme individualism. In this, of course, it is but reflecting the viewpoint of the members of the liberal-minded upper middle class who send their children to the Progressive schools. . . .

If Progressive Education is to be genuinely progressive, it must emancipate itself from the influence of this class, face squarely and courageously every social issue, come to grips with life in all of its stark reality, establish an organic relation with the community, develop a realistic and comprehensive theory of welfare, fashion a compelling and challenging vision of human destiny, and become less frightened than it is today at the bogies of *imposition* and *indoctrination*. In a word, Progressive Education cannot place its trust in a child-centered school.

11. National Survey of the Education of Teachers (1933)

Efforts to improve schools invariably led to concern about recruitment and education of teachers. This multivolume nationwide study of teacher education by the U.S. Office of Education concentrated on the inadequate schooling of teachers, their lack of professional training, the high levels of teacher transiency, and the difficulties faced by teachers in rural areas and black schools.

From the data presented in this chapter concerning the age, sex, marital status, experience, and transiency of teachers in public schools in the United States some generalizations are apparent.

1. In 1930–31 American public schools were taught predominantly by young, unmarried women with little teaching experience and that little obtained in two or more different school systems.

2. Marked differences in the items presented in this chapter were disclosed among the States but the differences among sections of the country, between urban and rural areas and among communities of different sizes were more significant than the differences among States.

3. Data presented on age, experience, and transiency of

SOURCE: U.S. Office of Education, *National Survey of the Education of Teachers*, Bulletin #10 (Washington, D.C.: U.S. Government Printing Office, 1933), Vol. 2, pp. 38–39; Vol. 4, pp. 11–13, 65–73.

teachers indicate very conclusively that the rural schools have suffered a serious educational handicap because they have had to take young teachers for their first teaching experience and then were unable to retain the services of those teachers after they had gained their initial experience at the expense of the rural children.

4. Transiency and its resultant "turnover" among teachers was caused largely by teachers moving to positions in larger communities and from elementary schools to secondary schools.

5. The minimum age at which persons may be certificated to teach is so low in many States that both inadequate preparation and transiency are encouraged.

6. Seven-eighths of all rural teachers in 1930–31 were women. Nineteen-twentieths of all other elementary teachers, three-fourths of the junior high school, and nearly two-thirds of the senior high school teachers were women.

7. The fact that the medians for teaching experience were in nearly all instances very much closer to the first quartiles of the distributions of experience than to the third quartile indicates that there was a heavy loss of young teachers. This fact may also be taken as an indication that teaching is not considered by many of the young people entering it as a permanent career. To the extent that teaching is regarded as a "stepping stone" or "stopgap" occupation, its progress toward professional status is definitely retarded.

8. The fact that transiency among teachers was greatest in rural schools and small communities indicates the need for programs of equalization of educational opportunities, with special attention to the improvement of working conditions for teachers in rural and village schools.

*   *   *

At the time the Survey was proposed many problems involved in the education of teachers were especially troublesome. They were in most cases of relatively recent origin, and this prevented those responsible for their solution from securing either guidance from past solutions or comfort from the knowledge that many other institutions had the same problems.

Frequently these problems were also so entangled with other problems that was impossible to locate exactly the elements in need of correction. For example, whether the curriculum for the education of an elementary teacher should comprise 2 years of general or nonprofessional work followed by 2 years of professional training was a question that could not be satisfactorily answered without having answers to such questions as: Is such a curriculum better than one in which the 4 years are given over to professionally presented subject-matter courses especially designed for elementary teachers? Will the certification laws permit the graduate of such a course to teach in another type of school, for example, in a high school? Do the salary schedules in the area served by the institution encourage 4 years of preparation for elementary teachers or do they justify only 2 or 3 years? Is the institution large enough to provide fully differentiated courses for elementary teachers? Are the instructors qualified to teach the professionally motivated courses and are they sympathetically inclined toward such courses?

Another problem which confronted all institutions educating teachers was the place and amount of practice teaching in the education of teachers for different types of teaching positions. Obviously a satisfactory answer to this question could not be obtained without knowing the answers to such questions as: What is the minimum degree of teaching skill required by the beginning teacher to protect him against initial failure because of preventable classroom mistakes? Should the minimum degree of teaching skill required vary according to the amount of supervision which is provided for beginning teachers? Is the same degree of initial teaching skill needed by high-school teachers as is needed by elementary teachers or by rural school teachers? What is the relative value of directed observation as compared with practice teaching in the development of initial teaching skill? Should practice teaching be given in one concentrated period or distributed at different times throughout the period of preparation, and if distributed, what are the most effective times to give it?

A third one of the entangled problems which faced presidents and faculty curriculum committees especially with regard to the preparation of high-school teachers was the number of fields in which prospective teachers should be prepared to teach. Involved in this question were such other questions as: What is the minimum amount of work in each field which is considered satisfactory preparation for teaching that field in a high school? How many subjects are high-school teachers generally required to teach and how does the number vary by size of high school and by subjects taught? What percent of beginning high-school teachers have to start their teaching experience in small high schools? Should the allotment of time to major and minor fields of specialization be made in terms of the requirements of the first few years of teaching experience during which the teacher will probably teach two, three, or more than three subjects or in terms of the fact that the majority of high-school teachers teach only one or two subjects? What differences in major and minor requirements must be made for such special subjects as music and art which require in addition to a command of the subject matter of a field, the development of skill in the techniques of the field?

A fourth illustration of the complicated problems which were attracting the attention of those responsible for the education of teachers and also of taxpayers and school patrons was the minimum of educational preparation which would be accepted for entrance into teaching at the different school levels. For example, was it satisfactory to allow graduates of high-school training classes to teach in the rural schools, require 2 or 3 years of preparation on the college level for elementary teachers in the villages and cities and require at least graduation from a standard college for all high-school teachers? Interwoven with this problem were such related questions as: What are the existing certification standards for the different school levels in the States and are those standards set by legal enactment or by State board regulations? Can a sufficient number of persons be secured to take the additional training if standards are raised and will the quality of recruits be affected adversely? Can standards for rural and elementary teachers be raised without greatly increasing the cost of public education? Is there any evidence to indicate that elementary teachers with 4 or more years of preparation above the high school are more effective teachers than those with only 2 years of such preparation? . . .

The data gathered by the Survey on the amount of educational preparation of American teachers and the discussions in this chapter and in the other volumes of the report have contributed to . . . a realization that the situation is unsatisfactory and the determination that something should be done to better it. . . . Unless otherwise specified it is understood that the proposed changes would be initiated, organized, and controlled by the regularly constituted educational authorities of the several States and that the necessary modifications would be made by each State to fit existing legal, educational, social, and financial conditions.

Most of these recommendations are for immediate action (by law or by State board regulations).

1. The amount of educational preparation required by all new teachers should equal or exceed the present generally accepted minimum standards of 2 years of college work beyond the completion of a standard high school for teachers in the elementary and rural schools and 4 years of college work for teachers in the secondary schools. . . .

2. Besides making sure that all new teachers have the desired minimum of educational preparation it is equally necessary to provide that all teachers now in service shall, by a fixed date, meet the same minimum requirements. . . .

3. In the States and cities in which separate schools are maintained for Negroes equal standards should be approved for the education of Negro teachers as are accepted for the education of white teachers. This means equivalence in the amount and quality of the work, but not necessarily identity of content for areas in which present conditions differ for the two races.

(a) Immediate attention should be given to the replacement or upgrading of the large group of Negro elementary teachers (22.5 percent) with no more than a high-school education.

(b) Immediate provision should also be made for the in-service upgrading of Negro elementary and secondary teachers whose educational preparation is less than the minimum standards of at least 2 years of college work for elementary and 4 years for secondary teachers.

4. State programs for the equalization of educational opportunities and for the more equitable distribution of the burden of the support of public education should include the teacher's preparation as one of the elements in the basic formula upon which such programs are based. . . .

5. Wherever satisfactory provisions for security of tenure, adequate salaries, and retirement allowances have not been made, these elements should be introduced into State and city programs in order that their effect upon the permanency of teaching as a profession may be utilized in raising standards.

6. Provision for the upgrading of teachers in service should not be concerned entirely with the removal of the group of teachers at the low end of the distribution of educational preparation. Encouragement to secure additional educational equipment should be given to all teachers in service even if they have met the accepted minimum standards. Upgrading which affects the entire group makes progress much more rapid than when only the lowest part of the group is affected.

7. States should sponsor programs to inform school-board members as to the possibilities, during periods of financial depression, of increasing standards for the edu-

cational preparation of teachers without increasing costs and in some instances even with decreased costs. . . .

It is probably wise, at the beginning of the discussion, to bring up the question which is raised more frequently than any other, namely, "Are there any distinctive elements in the education of a teacher which are not found in the education of any well-educated person?" This question in various guises is asked frequently by uninformed persons, by taxpayers intent upon reducing taxes, by enthusiastic teachers who are anxious to have as much of the student's time as possible, and by a few others not yet convinced that the science and art of teaching have developed to a degree which justifies including professional elements in the prospective teacher's preservice education.

Even though the question is raised frequently there is little doubt in the minds of most citizens and none in the minds of most teachers that a teacher does need to know something about the place of the school in society, the nature of the children being taught, the difficulties in learning the different subjects, the most effective methods of presenting certain information or of developing certain skills, the standards of accomplishment which should be expected, the methods of adjusting school work to individual needs and similar information which is distinct from the knowledge of the specific subject taught. Given the chance to choose between a teacher who knows those professional matters and one who does not — other things being equal — there would never be any doubt as to the selection. The question is, therefore, not whether a teacher should have special preparation for his work but instead, what he should have, how much he should have, and when he should have it. Too frequently

the question is put in a form which confuses the issue as
when some biased enthusiast states, "If I had to choose
between a teacher who has a scholarly knowledge of his
subject but has had no instruction in how to teach it and
one who has a thorough knowledge of how to teach his
subject but does not know his subject, I'd choose the
first." Of course, the only answer needed on such an
occasion is, "Who wouldn't?" If the issue is put as a
choice between all subject matter or all method there can
be only one answer if for no other reason than that it is
impossible effectively to study and master methods of
teaching a subject without a knowledge of the subject
matter to be taught. Fortunately the choice does not have
to be between the extreme points of this issue. If a
straight line represents at one of its extremities "all subject matter and no methods," at the other, "no subject
matter and all methods" and the points between the extremities proportional blends of subject matter and methods the solution of this issue can be at any one of the
infinite number of points which make up the line. There
is little doubt in the minds of most students of the problems of educating teachers that the solution should be at
a point distinctly toward the subject-matter end of the
line.

12. The Eight-Year Study (1933–1941)

*In an attempt to stimulate innovation in high school cur-
riculum and teaching, the Progressive Education Associa-*

SOURCE: Wilford M. Aiken, *Thirty Schools Tell Their Story* (New
York: McGraw-Hill, 1943), pp. 213–219, 226–229. Reprinted by permission of the publisher.

tion organized the Eight-Year Study. *Thirty public and private secondary schools were invited to participate in the experiment, and over 300 colleges agreed to waive their formal admissions requirements for those participating. The excerpt printed here, reporting on Des Moines, Iowa, reveals both the enthusiasm and the difficulties experienced as educators tried to change their philosophies and practices.*

In the spring of 1933 the Des Moines school system was invited to participate in the Eight-Year Study. Superintendent J. W. Studebaker accepted the invitation and held several meetings with teachers and supervisors representing various subjects to get their ideas of the kind of secondary school curriculum they would set up if they had considerable freedom to experiment. Out of these discussions came a plan for an experimental curriculum which would take half of the student's time and would be an integration of English and social studies, with science and the fine arts brought into the course as opportunities presented themselves. Theodore Roosevelt High School was selected to develop this course because a large number of its graduates continue their education in college. The original plan called for a study of world civilizations in the tenth grade, our American heritage in the eleventh, and personal and social problems in the twelfth. The tenth and eleventh grade courses included the reading of literature related to the social studies phase of the experimental curriculum, and opportunities to develop skill in oral and written expression. The twelfth grade course was divided into two parts: American Problems and Practical Problems of Living. The first consisted of a problem approach to the study of civics and economics; the second

consisted of four short courses of nine weeks each, dealing with personal and family relations, building and
financing a home, business practices, and personal problems in English. . . .

From the beginning of the experiment, pupil growth in
desirable traits was uppermost in the minds of teachers.
This is evident in the fact that descriptive reports of
progress toward certain desirable abilities, attitudes, and
skills were substituted for traditional marks. The cooperating teachers almost immediately recognized that they
did not have data adequate for making such reports, and
that these objectives would be sought with real earnest-
ness only if they were kept constantly before the minds of
all concerned. This created the necessity of evolving new
types of classroom procedures, new instruments of evaluation, and new types of records. . . .

Hence the most significant change that came about
during the entire course of the experiment was the shift
from subject matter to pupil needs as the criteria for the
selection of content. . . . While the shift is far from complete and there is still confusion as to a valid interpreta-
tion of pupil needs (immediate or deferred, personal or
social, cultural or practical), the acceptance of this view
points the way to a resolution of one of the major difficulties faced during the experimentation. The idea of an
experience or activity curriculum has grown and this philosophy has helped to resolve the conflict. The germs of
both the "child-centered school" and the "experience curriculum" were presented in the original planning, but it
took a number of years and a somewhat painful struggle
to bring them into their present stage of development. . . .

Among the problems confronted in the experimentation were a number which arose out of the fact that education is carried on by human beings and that the personal adjustments necessary for successful planning and the carrying out of plans are not always easy. The individual teacher had several such adjustments to make. He found it necessary to go through a continuous process of revising his philosophy of education, or at least of clarifying it; he found that as a consequence he must develop new criteria for the selection of content, new techniques of working with pupils or an increased emphasis on some techniques already partially in use, and new types of evaluation. He had to teach himself to place more responsibility on the individual child for the establishment of his own goals and for independent work in the achievement of those goals. Students had to be led to consider the teacher's role that of stimulating, guiding, or counseling rather than dictating, directing, judging. He had to see to it that the objectives of tolerance, understanding, and cooperativeness were possible of realization in his classroom. The great amount of time necessary for reading, thinking, planning, and preparing to handle the much wider range of materials and problems involved in the new curriculum was hard to find. So also was the time to evolve new types of records for new types of data. Not inconsiderable was the struggle to overcome the feeling of insecurity resulting from such changes. . . .

In a situation in which the experimentation is set up as only a part of the total school program with a limited number of students and teachers participating, there are sure to arise serious difficulties in securing the understanding and cooperation of nonparticipating faculty members. A very human and natural tendency which exhibited itself was due to a lack of understanding of the really tremendous amount of time and energy involved in doing experimental work. Teachers seeing other teachers with a so-called "free period," with special materials purchased for their classes, with time to attend meetings in other cities, often failed to realize that the "free period" was insufficient for the uses to which it was put. Some of these uses were: substituting for other teachers while they held planning conferences, arranging and managing a testing schedule, preparing reports of seniors for colleges, evolving and making new kinds of reports for students and parents, conferring with cooperating teachers and with curriculum assistants. These duties, however, seemed to others like special privileges instead of special responsibilities.

Too frequently their attitude was unfriendly, and hasty generalizations uncomplimentary to the whole experiment were based on the scanty evidence of one or two cases in which results were unsatisfactory rather than on the valuable contributions to the life of the whole school made by large numbers of students who were members of the experimental classes. It may be that this attitude was due to a jealousy springing from the assumption that those selected to do experimental work were considered better teachers than those not asked, or that a teacher's desire to do something different implied a reflection on the quality and effectiveness of performance of those not wishing to change. It is quite possible that the teachers concerned in experimentation did not, in the press of their almost overwhelming concern with their own immediate problems, take sufficient time or use enough tact in attempting to secure the sympathetic understanding of other faculty members. Certainly the experience in Roosevelt illustrated again the desirability of a more widespread participation in the process of changing the guiding educational philosophies and resulting procedures even at the cost of time. In that way many other teachers who were willing and eager to contribute to desirable change could have had their share in a more general plan of improvement.

13. High School and Life (1938)

One of the most prominent studies of secondary education during the 1930s, this survey of New York State high schools found them woefully lacking in curriculum, teaching, and, in particular, in providing adequate vocational training and vocational guidance. Like other studies of the period, the problems of youths once they left school became a critical reference point for what schools should be doing.

PREPARATION FOR VOCATION

At least three-fourths of the boys and girls who leave high school every year need to begin as soon as possible to earn their own livings. From the point of view of these boys and girls, quite as important as anything else the schools may do for them is the preparation the schools may give them for employment.

Boys and girls in a few of the large-city school sys-

SOURCE: Francis T. Spaulding, *High School and Life* (New York: McGraw-Hill, 1938), pp. 54–58. Reprinted by permission of the publisher.

tems in New York State can be sure of getting direct vocational preparation by enrolling in specialized vocational schools. The chance for a high school pupil to enter such a school is at present limited, however, both because only a few specialized schools have been established and because the number of pupils seeking admission to these schools is far greater than the number that can be accommodated. In most towns and cities all high school pupils attend comprehensive schools (in New York State traditionally called "academic high schools") which occasionally include vocational departments, but which provide core programs of general academic subjects. Inasmuch as these comprehensive schools are responsible for whatever vocational education is now supplied for the great majority of young people of high school age, the pupils from these schools, rather than the pupils from the specialized vocational schools, demand immediate consideration in any broad assessment of the vocational competence of New York State boys and girls.

VOCATIONAL PLANS OF PUPILS

The concern of the pupils in the academic high schools that their education should lead them somewhere vocationally has already been referred to. Widespread though it is, this concern does not seem to be accompanied by any realistic planning for jobs. Pupils' replies to questions about their vocational futures reveal that *large numbers of boys and girls on the point of leaving school either have no vocational plans or have plans which are quite out of line with their own demonstrated abilities and with opportunities for employment.*

From 17 to 40 per cent of the various groups of pupils

questioned had no long-range vocational objectives — no idea, that is to say, of the kinds of jobs they wanted to hold when they were finally through with school or college. The least uncertainty was found among the girls who were completing a year of postgraduate work in the high school; the greatest, among boys withdrawing before graduation. In general, the less successful a boy or girl had been in school, the vaguer he was about what he wanted to do vocationally.

Even more marked than their lack of long-range objectives was the uncertainty of the leaving pupils about their immediate jobs. Pupils who definitely intended to get jobs for the following year were questioned about their vocational chances as they saw them. The questions were asked in June of the pupils' last year in school — less than a month before they would actually be hunting for work. Pupils who had been "promised a job" or "knew of a job" were in the minority. Far more would commit themselves only to the statement that they thought they could get "some sort of job," or that they were uncertain whether they could get any job at all. Girls were in general less sure of their chances than boys. The graduates and post-graduates, despite the fact that they were the ones who most often had long-range objectives, tended to be less certain that they could get full-time jobs of the kinds they had specified than were the pupils who were leaving school without having graduated. . . . In spite of the lesson that an economic depression might be supposed to have taught them, relatively few pupils recognized that the lack of opportunities for actual jobs might have to be reckoned with.

The wisdom or lack of wisdom with which pupils were making their long-range plans was reflected also in the relation between their choices and the abilities they had shown in school. Pupils' vocational choices in general appeared to be geared roughly to their intelligence, the financial levels of their homes, and their school achievement. The pupils who ranked lowest in these measures more often hoped to be mechanics, commercial artists, beauticians, and bookkeepers; the pupils who ranked highest tended to choose such occupations as engineering, teaching, medicine, and the law. The inclination of all groups of pupils, however, was to choose much more frequently occupations at or approaching the professional levels than at lower levels, with the result that the number of choices at the upper levels was entirely out of proportion to present job opportunities. Furthermore, there was almost the widest possible range of choice among the pupils at any one level of ability, home background, or achievement. Large numbers of boys and girls of exceptional intellectual ability were looking forward to occupations which would never offer them a real challenge. Young people from homes ranking very low economically were often planning on careers which, if not quite out of the question from the financial standpoint, could be achieved in their cases only with extraordinary difficulty. Many pupils with mediocre or poor school records or with training in curricula offering no substantial basis for continued academic work, had in mind vocations which could be prepared for only by graduate study in a higher institution. Whatever degree of realistic wisdom was shown in the average choice of any large group of these pupils, individual unwisdom on the part of its members proved a more significant characteristic. . . .

It is not to be assumed that definiteness of vocational plans on the part of boys and girls about to leave school is either possible or desirable. The boy or girl who has not extraordinary ability, energy, and persistence is likely to be seriously handicapped by absolute definiteness of plan at a time when occupations are constantly shifting and vocational adaptability is more and more necessary. Young people's initial plans must necessarily be flexible if those plans are to be sensible, and every boy and girl must be ready to take advantage of opportunities which he may not have foreseen when he made his plans.

It is not to be assumed, either, that there should be complete agreement between pupils' aspirations and their eventual achievement. Vocational opportunities change, and individual futures may contain unexpected chances for success. Sometimes the change works disadvantageously: the boy or girl must be satisfied with a second best, or a tenth best, or any chance, if he is to get his feet on the ground economically. Partly because youth seems bound to be optimistic, partly because optimism is in itself a spur to success, there is not serious ground for disquiet in the fact that boys and girls aim somewhat above the mark which sober experience shows they are likely to attain.

But there is ground for disquiet in complete planlessness on the part of boys and girls who are face to face with the necessity of earning a living. There is ground for disquiet also in vocational ambitions which are not so much optimistic as thoroughly fantastic. There is ground for disquiet in young people's confident reliance on information about jobs which turns out to have been no information at all. Each of these weaknesses in their readiness to make a living is characteristic of large numbers of the boys and girls who are now leaving school in New York State.

14. Special Problems of Negro Education (1939)

By the end of 1930s, concern about the plight of black education was increasing. Black educator Doxey Wilkerson contrasted the sharp inequalities between the support given white and black Southern colleges, enumerated the difficult conditions facing Southern black school children, and argued that the educational inequities embedded in segregation undermined equality of educational opportunity.

The Southern Negro college stands at the apex of a system of school segregation. Experiencing directly the limitations characteristically imposed upon the Negro separate school, it suffers the further disadvantage of the cumulative deficiencies which it inherits in its students from inferior elementary and secondary schools. Yet, potentially, the Negro college occupies a position of vital importance to the welfare of both the Negro race and the country as a whole. From it should emanate that able and wholesome leadership so sorely needed by the Negro people. Further, in so far as the Negro college functions so as to aid the majority of Negroes to become better adjusted to the social and economic structure of the land, the strength of the Nation is significantly enhanced. . . .

SOURCE: Doxey A. Wilkerson, *Special Problems of Negro Education: Report of the Advisory Committee on Education* (Washington, D.C.: U.S. Government Printing Office, 1939), pp. 59, 72–74, 151–153. Reprinted by Negro Universities Press, 1970.

Publicly supported higher education for Negroes in the Southern States centers primarily in the land-grant colleges. There are two land-grant institutions in each of the Southern States, except the District of Columbia, one for white students and one for Negro students. The Negro land-grant institutions constitute slightly more than half of the public Negro institutions for higher education in these States. During 1937–38, they enrolled nearly three-fourths of the students in all public institutions of higher education for Negroes, and about one-third of the total in public and private institutions combined. In view of the predominant position of the land-grant colleges in public higher education for Negroes in the South and the further fact that these institutions are subsidized to a considerable extent by the Federal Government, it is appropriate for this inquiry to give special consideration to the scope of their educational programs, the size of their instructional staffs, and the financial support they receive. Directly comparable information for the white and Negro land-grant colleges in these States makes possible an appraisal of the relative adequacy of this important type of publicly supported higher education for the white and Negro populations of the South. . . .

In marked contrast with the varied educational programs afforded by the white land-grant colleges are the much more restricted programs of the Negro institutions. By far the predominant emphasis in all of the Negro land-grant colleges is teacher education. Slightly more than three-fifths of the resident students in these institutions take their majors in the arts and sciences or in education. The remainder are concentrated chiefly in the fields of agriculture, mechanic arts, and home economics, even here the chief emphasis being the preparation of teachers in these fields. With two exceptions . . . none of the Negro land-grant colleges offers any work whatever on the graduate level. Completely absent from their programs are curriculums in forestry, architecture, engineering, dentistry, pharmacy, medicine, law, library science, and journalism.

It is probable that limitations in the scope of educational programs in Negro land-grant colleges are, in some measure, imposed by deficiencies inherited from the inadequate public elementary and secondary school facilities for Negroes in the Southern States. Without doubt, another major factor—probably the chief cause—is the limited financial support given to the Negro institutions. However, regardless of factors contributing to the present situation, it is clear that, in the scope of their programs of resident instruction, considering educational levels as well as the variety of curriculum fields, the Negro land-grant colleges of the South afford opportunities for higher education which are far less comprehensive than those afforded by land-grant colleges for white students in the same States. . . .

The indexes utilized in this investigation point consistently, in practically every field, to a relatively low standard of public education for Negroes in the Southern States. In general, and especially in rural areas, Negro elementary pupils attend extremely impoverished, small, short-term schools, lacking in transportation service, void of practically every kind of instructional equipment, and staffed by relatively unprepared, overloaded teachers whose compensation does not approximate a subsistence wage. The vast majority of pupils progress through only the primary grades of these schools. The few who finish the elementary grades find relatively little opportunity, especially in rural areas, for a complete standard secondary education. Opportunities for education in public undergraduate colleges are even more limited, and opportunities for graduate and professional study at publicly controlled institutions are almost nonexistent. In most special and auxiliary educational programs and services — public libraries, vocational education, vocational rehabilitation, agricultural research, and agricultural and home economics extension — the same low standards obtain. Only in the case of one or two Federal emergency programs is there an approach to proportional provision of public education for Negroes in these States.

Educational opportunities in all fields are much more nearly adequate for the white population. Though its status is far below that for the Nation as a whole, still, on a scale of relative adequacy, public education for white persons in these [Southern] States is markedly superior to that for Negroes. For example, the general elementary and secondary schools for white children, as measured by per capita expenditures alone, function on a level which is approximating two and one-half times as high as that for corresponding Negro schools. The disparity between the general status of education for the two racial groups appears to be decreasing only very slowly, if at all. . . .

The most immediate effect of racial inequalities in public elementary and secondary education is reflected in the relative scholastic achievement of Negro children. There have been numerous studies of racial differences in scholastic achievement and their relationship to corresponding differences in school environment. They have demonstrated such facts as these: (1) That the extent of racial differences in scholastic achievement varies markedly among different school systems; (2) that such differences

are greater in segregated than in nonsegregated schools;
(3) that there is close correspondence between the extent
of racial differences in scholastic achievement and racial
differences in school environment; (4) that differences
between the achievement of white and Negro pupils in
Northern school systems are attributable almost entirely
to scholastic deficiencies on the part of Negro migrants
from impoverished school systems in the South; and (5)
that Negro graduates of Northern high schools maintain
better scholastic records in Southern Negro colleges than
do graduates of Southern Negro high schools. Such facts
as these afford one basis for appraising the effectiveness
of traditional programs of education for Negroes in separate schools.

15. Negro Youth in the Rural South (1941)

*Despite the inequities and the difficulties rural blacks
faced in going to school, sociologist Charles Johnson
found many blacks committed to education. Johnson's
pathbreaking work made clear how deeply embedded
faith in education had become and how poverty kept
many from attaining it.*

The results of our study indicate that the presumed
practical values of education have become a motivating
force for both parents and children to a remarkable de-

Source: Charles S. Johnson, *Growing Up in the Black Belt: Negro
Youth in the Rural South* (New York: Schocken Books, 1967; orig. pub.
1941), pp. 114–119. Reprinted by permission of the American Council
on Education.

gree, even in the plantation area. Their reasons were varied. Some wanted an education so they could "live in town," some "to make a living." One boy said, "Everybody needs to know how to read and count." The increased possibility of securing desirable work was perhaps most common. A 12-year-old seventh-grade Johnston County, North Carolina, girl, whose family is economically well-off according to community standards, thought, "Everybody ought to go to school and get educated. If you get a heap of schooling you get plenty of jobs when you finish." A 17-year-old tenth-grade Shelby County, Tennessee, boy said:

> I like school just fine because it tells you how to do the right thing at the right time. An education will tell you whether to farm this year or to do something else. . . .

Although many reasons for their interest in "schooling" were given, in general, education appears to have two vital meanings for most of these youth and their parents. First, education makes people literate. These people believe that their poverty is largely attributable to their inability to read and write. Hence, for them education meets an immediate, practical need. It protects them against frauds often practiced upon ignorant people who are tenant farmers. . . .

A Bolivar County, Mississippi, tenant farmer said:

> Children need all the education they can get and ought to get enough to keep people from cheating them. They should go through high school, and farther if they can. Especially the boys; they is the ones that need the education, 'cause they has to make a living.

Secondly, education is regarded as a means of escape from the prospect of an unpleasant occupation which is frequently associated in the minds of Negroes with a low racial status. The hope that education may offer a way of escape is expressed by a deserted, sharecropper mother of six children.

> I plan to let the children keep on in school as long as they want, until they want to leave. It sure is hard, but I'm willin' to struggle along to help them all I can. If a child ain't got a good education now days it be mighty hard on them. If I'd had more of it I wouldn't be so hard put now. I went to the sixth and had to come out to work. I don't know nothin' but farmin' and it's hard makin' a livin' on the farm. My girl is the oldest and I'm goin' to help her stay in school. She's smart, too.

A 16-year-old eighth-grade plantation girl of Macon County, Alabama, commented:

> I'd rather go to school than farm. I really like school. My folks are going to try and send me to Tuskegee and I want to go, too. It costs a lot of money and I can't say I'll get to go, but I sure do want to go, for I'd rather do anything than farm, and if I go to school I can do something else.

Another youth said, "Everybody ought to have an education. If you don't have an education, you'll have to work on a farm all the time." . . .

Although the hostile, indifferent "folk" attitudes toward education are rapidly giving way in the face of new conditions, need for the children's labor not infrequently is rationalized in terms of a lack of need for education. This attitude appeared most frequently in areas within the shadow of the plantation. An interesting example of this attitude appears in the comment of a struggling, illiterate sharecropper in Bolivar County who has seven children, all but one of whom are illiterate.

I ain't so worried 'bout my children getting all this schooling. They ain't going to do nothing nohow but work on the farm. I'll send them upon consideration up to the sixth grade, then they got to come out and help me. I went as high as the seventh, but it didn't do me no good. Unless you can go on to college, schooling ain't no 'count. My children just as well be home as chasing over there to that school house wastin' time and money.

3

Educational Excellence
in a Democratic Society
1942–1963

16. Elmtown's Youth (1941–1942)

In this excerpt from his study of the impact of social class on adolescents in a large Midwestern town, August Hollingshead discusses the powerful role extracurricular activities played in what the community expected from its high school.

An elaborate extracurricular program brings the school's activities before the public on a broader front than its teaching functions do, since this, the "circus side" of school, entertains students, parents, and Elmtowners in their leisure time. The entertainment features are emphasized by the Board of Education, the Superintendent, the principal, teachers, and students. They want their athletic teams to win games, their musical organizations to perform publicly at all possible times in a creditable manner, and their dramatics group to produce plays that will not be criticized but enjoyed. Extracurricular activities without spectator appeal or broad public relations value, such as girls' athletics, student government, and departmental clubs, receive little active support from the Board or the community.

ATHLETICS. There is far more public interest in the football and basketball teams than in all other high school

SOURCE: August B. Hollingshead, *Elmtown's Youth: The Impact of Social Classes on Adolescents* (New York: John Wiley & Sons, 1949), pp. 192–194. © 1949 by John Wiley & Sons, Inc. Reprinted by permission of John Wiley & Sons, Inc.

activities combined. The team has come to be a collective representation of the high school to a large segment of the community. Business, professional, and working men not only expect but also demand that the Board and the Superintendent hire a coach who can develop winning teams. The Superintendent knows he will be judged publicly in large part by the number of games the team wins in their contests with neighboring communities. The Board pays the maximum salary to the coach, and it expects him "to deliver the goods." A coach knows his "success" is determined wholly by the number of games he wins — particularly in basketball and football. . . .

During the basketball season, enthusiasm mounts until it reaches crescendo in the three-game series between the Elmtown Indians and their arch rivals, the Diamond City Jewels. A coach may lose the majority of the games played with other schools in the sports circuit, but if he loses to the Jewels he knows that he will have to look for another job in a year or two. Furthermore, the Superintendent is faced with the problem of explaining the school's failure to the Board of Education, adult fans, and *The Bugle*. . . .

Community pride is the issue in basketball games. Elmtown is approximately two and one-half times larger than Diamond City, and it reflects the usual belief in American culture that bigger is equivalent to better. Besides, Elmtown considers itself a "cleaner" town than Diamond City. Elmtowners for generations have associated immorality, vice, and crime with Diamond City. Thus, when the Indians and the Jewels meet on the athletic field more is at stake than winning or losing the game — particularly if the game is basketball.

The 1941–1942 sport season was disastrous for the Indians. They lost seven of the eight football games played, and one was to the Jewels. The three-game basketball series with Diamond City was a complete failure—the Indians lost every game. This was a galling load for the school authorities to bear; the school's critics seized upon these defeats as one more illustration of "incompetency" in the school. After the second defeat the desire to win the third game was so strong in some citizens that they offered rewards to the players before the game, if they won—theater tickets, merchandise, and in some cases money. One wealthy man offered a dollar a point to each boy who made a point; two fathers of team members added another dollar to the reward for each of their sons. Thus, these boys received two dollars for each point they made in the game. In the closing minutes of the third game, the referee called fouls on the Superintendent, the coach, and the Elmtown rooters; two team members were barred from the game for unnecessary roughness. One Elmtown boy knocked a Diamond City boy to the floor, and the referee sent him to the showers immediately. This cost his team two points, but one enthusiastic fan gave the boy five dollars after the game for his "good work."

17. The G.I. Bill of Rights (1944)

Passed in 1944 as part of the Servicemen's Readjustment Act, the G.I. Bill subsidized tuition, books, and fees and provided living expenses for 7.8 million veterans, almost 98 percent of whom were men. The veterans' extraordinary success furthered the expectation that higher education ought to be expanded, with some form of postsecondary schooling available to whomever wanted it.

2. Any such eligible person shall be entitled to education or training at an approved educational or training institution for a period of one year plus the time such person was in the active service on or after September 16, 1940, and before the termination of the war . . . *Provided*, That his work continues to be satisfactory throughout the period, according to the regularly prescribed standards and practices of the institution. . . .

3. (a) Such person shall be eligible for and entitled to such course of education or training, full time or the equivalent thereof in part-time training, as he may elect, and at any approved educational or training institution at which he chooses to enroll, whether or not located in the State in which he resides, which will accept or retain him as a student or trainee in any field or branch of knowledge which such institution finds him qualified to undertake or pursue. . . .

SOURCE: Eightieth Congress, 2d Session, House Committee Print No. 371 (1948).

5. The Administrator shall pay to the educational or training institution (including the institution offering institutional on-farm training), for each person enrolled in full time or part time course of education or training, the customary cost of tuition, and such laboratory, library, health, infirmary, and other similar fees as are customarily charged, and may pay for books, supplies, equipment, and other necessary expenses, exclusive of board, lodging, other living expenses, and travel, as are generally required for the successful pursuit and completion of the course by other students in the institution. . . .

11. As used in this part, the term "educational or training institutions" shall include all public or private elementary, secondary, and other schools furnishing education for adults, business schools and colleges, scientific and technical institutions, colleges, vocational schools, junior colleges, teachers colleges, normal schools, professional schools, universities, and other educational institutions, and shall also include business or other establishments providing apprentice or other training on the job. . . .

18. Community Colleges and Educational Opportunity (1947)

Appointed by President Harry S. Truman to examine "the functions of higher education in our democracy and the means by which they can best be performed," the Commission on Higher Education urged a major expansion of postsecondary schooling. Central to the furthering of educational opportunity, the Commission believed, were the community colleges, soon to become the fastest growing sector of higher education, whose mission was to serve local communities through adult learning, training for the skilled labor market, and preparation of students not yet ready to attend four-year institutions.

As one means of achieving the expansion of educational opportunity and the diversification of educational offerings it considers necessary, this Commission recommends that the number of community colleges be increased and that their activities be multiplied.

Community colleges in the future may be either publicly or privately controlled and supported, but most of them, obviously, will be under public auspices. They will be mainly local or regional in scope and should be locally controlled, though they should be carefully planned to fit into a comprehensive Statewide system of higher educa-

SOURCE: President's Commission on Higher Education, *Higher Education for American Democracy* (Washington: Government Printing Office, 1947), vol. 3, pp. 67–68.

tion. They will derive much of their support from the local community, supplemented by aid from State funds. Some community colleges may offer a full four years of college work, but most of them probably will stop at the end of the fourteenth grade, the sophomore year of the traditional college. In the latter case they should be closely articulated with the high school.

Whatever form the community college takes, its purpose is educational service to the entire community. . . . It will provide college education for the youth of the community certainly, so as to remove geographic and economic barriers to educational opportunity and discover and develop individual talents at low cost and easy access. But in addition, the community college will serve as an active center of adult education. It will attempt to meet the total post-high school needs of its community.

In the past the junior college has most commonly sought to provide within the local community the freshman and sophomore courses of the traditional college curriculum. With notable exceptions, it has concentrated on preparing students for further study in the junior and senior years of liberal arts colleges or professional schools.

But preparatory programs looking to the more advanced courses of the senior college are not complete and rounded in themselves, and they usually do not serve well the purposes of those who must terminate their schooling at the end of the fourteenth grade. Half the young people who go to college find themselves unable to complete the full 4-year course, and for a long time to come more students will end their formal education in the junior college years than will prolong it into the senior college. These 2-year graduates would gain more from a terminal program planned specifically to meet their needs than from the first half of a 4-year curriculum.

19. *Brown v. Board of Education of Topeka, Kansas* (1954)

In one of the most dramatic decisions in the history of American education, the Supreme Court unanimously ruled on May 17, 1954, that the "separate but equal" doctrine was unconstitutional and that the segregation by law of public school students was illegal. A year later, on May 31, 1955, the Court urged federal courts to act "to admit to public school on a racially nondiscriminatory basis with all deliberate speed the parties to these cases."

These cases come to us from the States of Kansas, South Carolina, Virginia, and Delaware. They are premised on different facts and different local conditions, but a common legal question justifies their consideration together in this consolidated opinion.

In each of the cases, minors of the Negro race, through their legal representatives, seek the aid of the courts in obtaining admission to the public schools of their community on a nonsegregated basis. In each instance, they had been denied admission to schools attended by white children under laws requiring or permitting segregation according to race. This segregation was alleged to deprive the plaintiffs of the equal protection of the laws under the

---

SOURCE: *Brown et al. v. Board of Education of Topeka, Kansas, et al.*, 347 U.S. 483 (1954).

Fourteenth Amendment. In each of the cases other than the Delaware case, a three-judge federal district court denied relief to the plaintiffs on the so-called "separate but equal" doctrine announced by this Court in *Plessy v. Ferguson*, 163 U.S. 537. Under that doctrine, equality of treatment is accorded when the races are provided substantially equal facilities, even though these facilities be separate. . . .

The plaintiffs contend that segregated public schools are not "equal" and cannot be made "equal," and that hence they are deprived of the equal protection of the laws. Because of the obvious importance of the question presented, the Court took jurisdiction. Argument was heard in the 1952 Term, and reargument was heard this Term on certain questions propounded by the Court.

Reargument was largely devoted to the circumstances surrounding the adoption of the Fourteenth Amendment in 1868. It covered exhaustively consideration of the Amendment in Congress, ratification by the states, then existing practices in racial segregation, and the views of proponents and opponents of the Amendment. This discussion and our own investigation convince us that, although these sources cast some light, it is not enough to resolve the problem with which we are faced. At best, they are inconclusive. The most avid proponents of the post-War Amendments undoubtedly intended them to remove all legal distinctions among "all persons born or naturalized in the United States." Their opponents, just as certainly, were antagonistic to both the letter and the spirit of the Amendments and wished them to have the most limited effect. What others in Congress and the state legislatures had in mind cannot be determined with any degree of certainty. . . .

In the first cases in this Court construing the Fourteenth Amendment, decided shortly after its adoption, the Court interpreted it as proscribing all state-imposed discriminations against the Negro race. The doctrine of "separate but equal" did not make its appearance in this Court until 1896 in the case of *Plessy v. Ferguson, supra,* involving not education but transportation. American courts have since labored with the doctrine for over half a century. In this Court, there have been six cases involving the "separate but equal" doctrine in the field of public education. In *Cumming v. County Board of Education,* 175 U.S. 528, and *Gong Lum v. Rice,* 275 U.S. 78, the validity of the doctrine itself was not challenged. In more recent cases, all on the graduate school level, inequality was found in that specific benefits enjoyed by white students were denied to Negro students of the same educational qualifications. *Missouri ex rel. Gaines v. Canada,* 305 U.S. 337; *Sipuel v. Oklahoma,* 332 U.S. 631; *Sweatt v. Painter,* 339 U.S. 629; *McLaurin v. Oklahoma State Regents,* 339 U.S. 637. In none of these cases was it necessary to re-examine the doctrine to grant relief to the Negro plaintiff. And in *Sweatt v. Painter, supra,* the Court expressly reserved decision on the question whether *Plessy v. Ferguson* should be held inapplicable to public education.

In the instant cases, that question is directly presented. Here, unlike *Sweatt v. Painter,* there are findings below that the Negro and white schools involved have been equalized, or are being equalized, with respect to buildings, curricula, qualifications and salaries of teachers, and other "tangible" factors. Our decision, therefore, cannot turn on merely a comparison of these tangible factors in the Negro and white schools involved in each of the cases. We must look instead to the effect of segregation itself on public education.

In approaching this problem, we cannot turn the clock back to 1868 when the Amendment was adopted, or even to 1896 when *Plessy v. Ferguson* was written. We must consider public education in the light of its full development and its present place in American life throughout the Nation. Only in this way can it be determined if segregation in public schools deprives these plaintiffs of the equal protection of the laws.

Today, education is perhaps the most important function of state and local governments. Compulsory school attendance laws and the great expenditures for education both demonstrate our recognition of the importance of education to our democratic society. It is required in the performance of our most basic public responsibilities, even service in the armed forces. It is the very foundation of good citizenship. Today it is a principal instrument in awakening the child to cultural values, in preparing him for later professional training, and in helping him to adjust normally to his environment. In these days, it is doubtful that any child may reasonably be expected to succeed in life if he is denied the opportunity of an education. Such an opportunity, where the state has undertaken to provide it, is a right which must be made available to all on equal terms.

We come then to the question presented: Does segregation of children in public schools solely on the basis of race, even though the physical facilities and other "tangible" factors may be equal, deprive the children of the minority group of equal educational opportunities? We believe that it does. . . .

To separate them from others of similar age and qualifications solely because of their race generates a feeling of inferiority as to their status in the community that may affect their hearts and minds in a way unlikely ever to be undone. . . . Whatever may have been the extent of psychological knowledge at the time of *Plessy v. Ferguson*, this finding is amply supported by modern authority. Any language in *Plessy v. Ferguson* contrary to this finding is rejected.

We conclude that in the field of public education the doctrine of "separate but equal" has no place. Separate educational facilities are inherently unequal.

20. Encouraging Scientific Talent (1956)

By the mid-1950s, concern about the United State's ability to meet the demands of a highly technological world and to compete with the Soviet Union led to a vigorous debate about the quality of American education. This study, sponsored by the College Entrance Examination Board, criticizes the insufficiency of schooling for the academically talented and urges educators to improve science and mathematics education.

To just what extent the nation's schools encourage scholarly endeavor is a matter of considerable current

SOURCE: Charles C. Cole, Jr., *Encouraging Scientific Talent: A Study of America's Able Students Who Are Lost to College and of Ways of Attracting Them to College and Science Careers* (New York: College Entrance Examination Board, 1956), pp. 113–115, 120–121. © 1956 by College Entrance Examination Board, New York. Reprinted with permission.

controversy. Critics of our public schools have condemned them for the products they turn out, for the inadequate teaching that is said to exist, for the superficiality instilled in the student, and for catering to the mediocre pupil at the expense of the superior one. Various aspects of current educational philosophy have been scrutinized by critics who have attacked John Dewey's influence, bewailed the wide variety of new subjects taught in the classroom, and denounced new pedagogical methods, particularly if they cost tax payers any money. The schools' defenders, on the other hand, have cited studies to show that today's pupils are better than yesterday's, are well informed, and can read and write much better than their predecessors 50 years ago. . . .

It is not our purpose to add fuel to this controversy. Many public and private schools at present are doing a difficult job very well and would do a better job if they had the means to do so. A number of schools are forced to offer curricula that are governed not by what they believe is educationally sound but by the limited means at hand. It is similarly not the fault of the schools that many of them are notoriously overcrowded and understaffed and that many face increasing numbers of pupils in the future. . . .

But while our schools are good, they could be better. Faced with more customers than ever before, the current approach, while appropriate and quite adequate for most students, is not excellent enough for those of high ability. . . . How is the public school handicapped in trying to identify and encourage its students of high ability? Unable to expand in staff or facilities as fast as its student body, the school has been swamped with too many children and has had to devote its major efforts to coping with sheer numbers. This has forced the school to adopt a system of education which was recently described as "an enormous, complicated machine for sorting and ticketing and routing children through life." As classes have grown, bright youngsters have received increasingly less individual attention and budding geniuses have without doubt been overlooked and neglected. Large class size puts a premium on standardization, and in a standardized program the interests of those with distinguished ability suffer. These students can coast along without much exertion and may never realize how much they could really accomplish if sufficiently challenged. Programs characterized by strong intellectual challenge, superior quality of instruction, and high standards can be potent stimulants to a scientific career while diluted curricula and uninspired teaching will often fail to develop potential scientists. . . .

Because of our dire shortage of persons with specialized ability and because of the early achievement levels in human beings, we must get away from the notion that there is something inherently bad or undemocratic about acceleration or the devising of special programs for the high ability student. We have fast and slow lanes in our highways. We accept the need for local and express trains. We recognize the existence of wide variations in physical strength and expect a strong man to carry more, leap higher, and run faster than a weak one. To force the rapid learner to mark time or to deprive the brilliant student of additional intellectual challenge is a waste of a natural resource, human talent. Once this has been wasted, it can never be retrieved. . . .

Another aspect of the schools obviously important in producing scientists is their course offerings in general and their science offerings in particular. The increasingly wide variety of nonacademic courses generally available for graduation credit that has stemmed from mass high school attendance bears directly on the recruitment of students for scientific careers. The many course options now available to students serve frequently to deter them from taking the high school mathematics, physics, and chemistry essential to a college science major. The new practical, interesting, and frequently helpful electives available to the high school students should not be disparaged in themselves. But it is unfortunate that young persons are most often not given sufficient information about their capabilities or guidance in selecting careers before they elect courses in driving an automobile, stenography, or consumer economics instead of the "harder" ones in trigonometry or physics. It may be fine to have high school students exercising freedom of choice in planning their programs, but their choices will not be truly free if the school cannot insure that they will be based on fairly full information. We should not expect the schools to curb the education of the many but we should help the schools to enhance the education of the few who can make a significant contribution to society if their intellectual capacities are fully developed.

21. Crisis in Education (1958)

The launching of Sputnik in October 1957 focused the criticisms of American education. The tone of the debate

SOURCE: Sloan Wilson, "The Crisis in Education," *Life Magazine*, March 24, 1958, pp. 25–28, 33. Reprinted by permission of the author.

was captured in a Life Magazine *series entitled "Crisis in Education" that stressed the sharp contrast between Soviet and U.S. schools and urged an end to "the waste of fine minds."*

For years most critics of U.S. education have suffered the curse of Cassandra—always to tell the truth, seldom to be listened to or believed. But now the curse has been lifted. What they were saying is beginning to be believed. The schools are in terrible shape. What has long been an ignored national problem, Sputnik has made a recognized crisis. . . .

- The schools have been overcrowded for years, but children still study in shacks and shifts and hallways and jerry-built classrooms.
- Most teachers are grossly underpaid (some are not worth what they get). A great many, who know their jobs well and practice them with devotion, have to work without help, understanding or proper tools.
- In their eagerness to be all things to all children, schools have gone wild with elective courses. They build up the bodies with in-school lunches and let the minds shift for themselves.
- Where there are young minds of great promise, there are rarely the means to advance them. The nation's stupid children get far better care than the bright. The geniuses of the next decades are even now being allowed to slip back into mediocrity.
- There is no general agreement on what the schools should teach. A quarter century has been wasted with

the squabbling over whether to make a child well adjusted or teach him something.

Most appalling, the standards of education are shockingly low.

Two 16-year-olds, Stephen Lapekas of Chicago and Alexei Kutzkov of Moscow, are getting what their own countries consider a good, standard public education. Stephen is an 11th-grader at Austin High, one of the city's finer high schools. Alexei is in his 10th and final year at Moscow School 49. But the difference in what they learn and the atmosphere in which they learn it measures the frightening scale of the problems the U.S. now faces in its public schools. . . .

Stephen is an average student, likable, considerate, good-humored — the kind of well-adjusted youngster U.S. public schools are proud of producing. Alexei is hardworking, aggressive, above average in his grades — the kind of student that the Russian system ruthlessly sets out to produce. For Stephen, the business of getting educated seldom seems too serious. For Alexei, who works in a much harsher intellectual climate, good marks in school are literally more important than anything else in his life.

Stephen hopes to go to college after he finishes at Austin High but knows future success does not depend entirely on this. Alexei is filled with a fierce determination to get to college and become a physicist. In Russia, which desperately needs trained manpower, few can rise above a humble level without a good education. The entire school system has been geared to this. With a curriculum standardized across the country and with no elective subjects, the Soviet 10-year schools are like mammoth obstacle courses for the nation's youth. The laggards are forced out by tough periodic examinations and shunted to less demanding trade schools and apprenticeships. Only a third — 1.4 million in 1957 — survive all 10 years and finish the course.

For all its laxness, the system under which Stephen studies does develop flexibility and, in Stephen, qualities of leadership. For all its stern virtues, the system under which Alexei studies develops rigidity and subservience to an undemocratic state. But there is no blinking at the educational results. Academically Alexei is two years ahead of Stephen. As one example, he has read Shakespeare and Shaw in literature class while Stephen has only just finished reading Stevenson's *Kidnapped*. . . .

Russian schools put a heavy emphasis on science and more than half of Alexei's classroom time is given over to scientific subjects. But Alexei also has a firm foundation in literature and languages. He has studied all the great Russian writers, including Tolstoy and Dostoevsky, and in his English classes English is spoken more often than Russian. Though the range and depth of the studies is impressive, there is one catch. Russian students learn a great deal by rote and seldom strike out to explore any subject on their own initiative beyond the material printed in their textbooks.

Though Alexei gets no direct political indoctrination in school, he is constantly reminded of his duties toward the state. Pictures and slogans of Lenin are few but conspicuous. The literature courses pay considerable attention to contemporary fiction which glorifies the Soviet way of life. Modern history, which Alexei is studying this year, emphasizes Russia's feats in World War II. For a year after Stalin's death Russian schools stopped giving examinations in modern history, while the party rewrote texts to include Stalin's "personal errors."

Alexei's teachers are well trained. They run their classes with a firm hand. Discipline has relaxed a little since Stalin's death, but pupils are still careful not to act up. If a student gets less than an A in behavior, school authorities can suggest pointedly that he reconsider his plans for applying to college. . . .

Classes at Austin are relaxed and enlivened by banter. For Stephen, who is taking an academic course, this year's subjects include English, American history, geometry and biology, respectable enough courses but on a much less advanced level than Alexei's. The intellectual application expected of him is moderate. In English, for instance, students seldom bother to read assigned books and sometimes make book reports based on comic book condensations. Stephen's extracurricular activities, in which he really shows talent and energy, leave him little time for hard study. He is the high school's star swimmer and a leader in student affairs. As a result, though the teachers consider him intelligent, he is behind in math and his grades are mediocre. "I worry about 'em," he admits, "but that's about as far as it goes."

22. National Defense Education Act (1958)

In response to the sense of crisis, Congress passed the National Defense Education Act in 1958. The Act greatly expanded the federal government's role in education through the provision of categorical aid to improve sci-

SOURCE: Public Law 85-864 (September 2, 1958).

ence, mathematics, and foreign language instruction. Federal funds were used to develop new curricula, improve teacher training and guidance, purchase science, mathematics, and foreign language equipment and materials, and, in an important decision, to provide fellowships and loans to college and postgraduate students.

Sec. 101. The Congress hereby finds and declares that the security of the Nation requires the fullest development of the mental resources and technical skills of its young men and women. The present emergency demands that additional and more adequate educational opportunities be made available. The defense of this Nation depends upon the mastery of modern techniques developed from complex scientific principles. It depends as well upon the discovery and development of new principles, new techniques, and new knowledge.

We must increase our efforts to identify and educate more of the talent of our Nation. This requires programs that will give assurance that no student of ability will be denied an opportunity for higher education because of financial need; will correct as rapidly as possible the existing imbalances in our educational programs which have led to an insufficient proportion of our population educated in science, mathematics, and modern foreign languages and trained in technology.

The Congress reaffirms the principle and declares that the States and local communities have and must retain control over and primary responsibility for public education. The national interest requires, however, that the Federal Government give assistance to education for programs which are important to our defense.

Sec. 102. Nothing contained in this Act shall be construed to authorize any department, agency, officer, or employee of the United States to exercise any direction, supervision, or control over the curriculum, program of instruction, administration, or personnel of any educational institution or school system. . . .

Sec. 201. For the purpose of enabling the Commissioner to stimulate and assist in the establishment at institutions of higher education of funds for the making of low-interest loans to students in need thereof to pursue their courses of study in such institutions, there are hereby authorized to be appropriated $47,500,000 for the fiscal year ending June 30, 1959, $75,000,000 for the fiscal year ending June 30, 1960, $82,500,000 for the fiscal year ending June 30, 1961, $90,000,000 for the fiscal year ending June 30, 1962, and such sums for the fiscal year ending June 30, 1963, and each of the three succeeding fiscal years as may be necessary to enable students who have received a loan for any school year ending prior to July 1, 1962, to continue or complete their education. . . .

(b) Loans from any such loan fund to any student by any institution of higher education shall be made on such terms and conditions as the institution may determine; subject, however, to such conditions, limitations, and requirements as the Commissioner may prescribe . . . except that—

(1) such a loan shall be made only to a student who (A) is in need of the amount of the loan to pursue a course of study at such institution, and (B) is capable, in the opinion of the institution, of maintaining good standing in such course of study, and (C) has been accepted for enrollment as a full-time student at such institution or, in the case of a student already attending

such institution, is in good standing and in full-time attendance there either as an undergraduate or graduate student; . . .

(3) not to exceed 50 per centum of any such loan (plus interest) shall be canceled for service as a full-time teacher in a public elementary or secondary school in a State, at the rate of 10 per centum of the amount of such loan plus interest thereon . . .

(4) such a loan shall bear interest, on the unpaid balance of the loan, at the rate of 3 per centum per annum except that no interest shall accrue before the date on which repayment of the loan is to begin; . . .

Sec. 301. There are hereby authorized to be appropriated $70,000,000 for the fiscal year ending June 30, 1959, and for each of the three succeeding fiscal years, for (1) making payments to State educational agencies under this title for the acquisition of equipment (suitable for use in providing education in science, mathematics, or modern foreign language). . . .

Sec. 403. (a) The Commissioner shall award fellowships under this title to individuals accepted for study in graduate programs approved by him under this section.

23. The Process of Education (1960)

Professor of Psychology at Harvard University, Jerome Bruner captured the excitement of the curriculum reform movement of the late 1950s and early 1960s. Bruner was

SOURCE: Jerome S. Bruner, *The Process of Education* (Cambridge: Harvard University Press, 1977; orig. pub. 1960) pp. xvii–xviii, 18–19, 33, 52–54, 69–70. Copyright © 1960, 1977 by the President and Fellows of Harvard College. Reprinted by permission.

especially interested in matching the structure of academic disciplines with the student's emerging conceptual and developmental abilities to create innovative curricula and new approaches to teaching.

Something new was stirring in the land. A tour of the United States in the summer of 1959 would have revealed a concentration of distinguished mathematicians in Boulder, Colorado, engaged in writing new textbooks for primary, junior high, and high school grades. In Kansas City, there could be found a group of first-class biologists busily producing films on subjects such as the structure of the cell and photo-synthesis for use in tenth-grade biology courses. In Urbana, Illinois, there was a flurry of work on the teaching of fundamental mathematical concepts to grade-school children, and in Palo Alto one might have found a mathematical logician at work trying out materials for teaching geometry to children in the beginning grades of school. In Cambridge, Massachusetts, work was progressing on an "ideal" physics course for high school students, engaging the efforts not only of text writers and film producers but also of men who had earned world renown in theoretical and experimental physics. At various centers throughout the country, teachers were being trained to teach this new physics course by others who had already tried it. Preliminary work was under way in Boulder on a junior high school course in biology, and a group of chemists were similarly engaged in their field in Portland, Oregon. Various learned societies were searching for and finding ways of establishing contact between their leading scholars and educators in the schools. For their part, educators and psychologists were examining anew the nature of teaching methods and curricula and were becoming increasingly ready to examine fresh approaches. (pp. xvii–xviii)

The first and most obvious problem is how to construct curricula that can be taught by ordinary teachers to ordinary students and that at the same time reflect clearly the basic or underlying principles of various fields of inquiry. The problem is twofold: first, how to have the basic subjects rewritten and their teaching materials revamped in such a way that the pervading and powerful ideas and attitudes relating to them are given a central role; second, how to match the levels of these materials to the capacities of students of different abilities at different grades in school.

The experience of the past several years has taught at least one important lesson about the design of a curriculum that is true to the underlying structure of its subject matter. It is that the best minds in any particular discipline must be put to work on the task. The decision as to what should be taught in American history to elementary school children or what should be taught in arithmetic is a decision that can best be reached with the aid of those with a high degree of vision and competence in each of these fields. To decide that the elementary ideas of algebra depend upon the fundamentals of the commutative, distributive, and associative laws, one must be a mathematician in a position to appreciate and understand the fundamentals of mathematics. Whether school children require an understanding of Frederick Jackson Turner's ideas about the role of the frontier in American history before they can sort out the facts and trends of American history—this again is a decision that requires the help of the scholar who has a deep understanding of the American past. Only by the use of our best minds in devising curricula will we bring the fruits of scholarship and wisdom to the student just beginning his studies. (pp. 18–19).

We begin with the hypothesis that any subject can be taught effectively in some intellectually honest form to any child at any stage of development. It is a bold hypothesis and an essential one in thinking about the nature of a curriculum. (p. 33)

If one respects the ways of thought of the growing child, if one is courteous enough to translate material into his logical forms and challenging enough to tempt him to advance, then it is possible to introduce him at an early age to the ideas and styles that in later life make an educated man. We might ask, as a criterion for any subject taught in primary school, whether, when fully developed, it is worth an adult's knowing, and whether having known it as a child makes a person a better adult. If the answer to both questions is negative or ambiguous, then the material is cluttering the curriculum.

If the hypothesis with which this section was introduced is true — that any subject can be taught to any child in some honest form — then it should follow that a curriculum ought to be built around the great issues, principles, and values that a society deems worthy of the continual concern of its members. Consider two examples — the teaching of literature and of science. If it is granted, for example, that it is desirable to give children an awareness of the meaning of human tragedy and a sense of compassion for it, is it not possible at the earliest appropriate age to teach the literature of tragedy in a manner that illuminates but does not threaten? There are many possible ways to begin: through a retelling of the great myths, through the use of children's classics, through presentation of and commentary on selected films that have proved themselves. Precisely what kinds of materials should be used at what age with what effect is a subject for research — research of several kinds. We may ask first about the child's conception of the tragic, and here one might proceed in much the same way that Piaget and his colleagues have proceeded in studying the child's conception of physical causality, of morality, of number, and the rest. It is only when we are equipped with such knowledge that we will be in a position to know how the child will translate whatever we present to him into his own subjective terms. Nor need we wait for all the research findings to be in before proceeding, for a skillful teacher can also experiment by attempting to teach what seems to be intuitively right for children of different ages, correcting as he goes. In time, one goes beyond to more complex versions of the same kind of literature or simply revisits some of the same books used earlier. What matters is that later teaching build upon earlier reactions to literature, that it seek to create an ever more explicit and mature understanding of the literature of tragedy. Any of the great literary forms can be handled in the same way, or any of the great themes — be it the form of comedy or the theme of identity, personal loyalty, or what not.

So too in science. If the understanding of number, measure, and probability is judged crucial in the pursuit of science, then instruction in these subjects should begin as intellectually honestly and as early as possible in a manner consistent with the child's forms of thought. Let the topics be developed and redeveloped in later grades. Thus, if most children are to take a tenth-grade unit in biology, need they approach the subject cold? Is it not possible, with a minimum of formal laboratory work if necessary, to introduce them to some of the major biological ideas earlier, in a spirit perhaps less exact and more intuitive? (pp. 52–54)

The efforts of the past decade began with the modest intention of doing a better job of teaching physics or mathematics or some other subject. The impulse that led a group of highly competent physicists, for example, to join together in this effort was the sense of how great a gap had developed between physics as known by the physicist and physics as taught in school, a gap of particular importance because of revolutionary advances in science and the crisis in national security. But as the effort broadened, as scholars and scientists from other disciplines entered the field, a broader objective began to emerge. It is clear that there is in American education today a new emphasis upon the pursuit of excellence. There appear to be several things implied by the pursuit of excellence that have relevance not only to what we teach, but to how we teach and how we arouse the interest of our students.

The view has already been expressed that the pursuit of excellence must not be limited to the gifted student. But the idea that teaching should be aimed at the average student in order to provide something for everybody is an equally inadequate formula. The quest, it seems to many of us, is to devise materials that will challenge the superior student while not destroying the confidence and will-to-learn of those who are less fortunate. We have no illusions about the difficulty of such a course, yet it is the only one open to us if we are to pursue excellence and at the same time honor the diversity of talents we must educate. (pp. 69–70)

24. The Multiversity (1963)

In what quickly became a highly controversial statement about the purposes of higher education, the President of the University of California claimed that the search for knowledge was fundamentally reshaping the university and its relationship to American society. University activities, Clark Kerr argued, now encompassed almost every conceivable social aim, making higher education more central to the national purpose than ever before.

The basic reality, for the university, is the widespread recognition that new knowledge is the most important factor in economic and social growth. We are just now perceiving that the university's invisible product, knowledge, may be the most powerful single element in our culture, affecting the rise and fall of professions and even of social classes, of regions and even of nations.

Because of this fundamental reality, the university is being called upon to produce knowledge as never before—for civic and regional purposes, for national purposes, and even for no purpose at all beyond the realization that most knowledge eventually comes to serve mankind. And it is also being called upon to transmit knowledge to an unprecedented proportion of the population.

Source: Clark Kerr, *The Uses of the University* (Cambridge: Harvard University Press, 1982; orig. pub. 1963), pp. vii–ix, 18–19, 27, 42, 52–53. Copyright © 1963, 1982 by the President and Fellows of Harvard College. Reprinted by permission.

This reality is reshaping the very nature and quality of the university. Old concepts of faculty-student relations, of research, of faculty-administration roles are being changed at a rate without parallel. And this at a time when it seems that an entire generation is pounding at the gates and demanding admission. To the academician, conservative by nature, the sound made by the new generation often resembles the howl of a mob. To the politician, it is a signal to be obeyed. To the administrator, it is a warning that we are in new times and that the decisions we make now will be uncommonly productive — both of good and ill.

Thus the university has come to have a new centrality for all of us, as much for those who never see the ivied halls as for those who pass through them or reside there. (pp. v–vii)

The multiversity is an inconsistent institution. It is not one community but several — the community of the undergraduate and the community of the graduate; the community of the humanist, the community of the social scientist, and the community of the scientist; the communities of the professional schools; the community of all the nonacademic personnel; the community of the administrators. Its edges are fuzzy — it reaches out to alumni, legislators, farmers, businessmen, who are all related to one or more of these internal communities. As an institution, it looks far into the past and far into the future, and is often at odds with the present. It serves society almost slavishly — a society it also criticizes, sometimes unmercifully. Devoted to equality of opportunity, it is itself a class society. A community, like the medieval communities of masters and students, should have common interests; in the multiversity, they are quite varied, even conflicting. A community should have a soul, a single animating principle; the multiversity has several—some of them quite good, although there is much debate on which souls really deserve salvation. (pp. 18–19)

When "the borders of the campus are the boundaries of our state," the lines dividing what is internal from what is external become quite blurred; taking the campus to the state brings the state to the campus. In the so-called "private" universities, alumni, donors, foundations, the federal agencies, the professional and business communities bulk large among the semi-external influences; and in the so-called "public" universities, the agricultural, trade union, and public school communities are likely to be added to the list, and also a more searching press. The multiversity has many "publics" with many interests; and by the very nature of the multiversity many of these interests are quite legitimate and others are quite frivolous. (p. 27)

The multiversity is in the main stream of events. To the teacher and the researcher have been added the consultant and the administrator. Teaching is less central than it once was for most faculty members; research has become more important. This has given rise to what has been called the "non-teacher"—the higher a man's standing, the less he has to do with students. (p. 42)

Currently, federal support has become a major factor in the total performance of many universities, and the sums involved are substantial. Higher education in 1960 received about $1.5 billion from the federal government—a hundredfold increase in twenty years. About one third of this $1.5 billion was for university-affiliated research centers; about one third for project research within universities; about one third for other things, such as residence hall loans, scholarships, and teaching programs. This last third was expended at colleges as well as universities, but the first two thirds almost exclusively at universities, and at relatively few of them.

The $1 billion for research, though only 10 percent of total federal support for research and development, accounted for 75 percent of all university expenditures on research and 15 percent of total university budgets. Clearly the shape and nature of university research are profoundly affected by federal monies. (pp. 52–53)

4

The Expansion of Opportunity
1964–1980

25. Elementary and Secondary Education Act (1965)

Passed on April 9, 1965, less than three months after it was introduced, ESEA was the most important educational component of the "war on poverty." Title I, which received almost 80 percent of the $1.25 billion initially allocated, was designed to meet the "special educational needs of educationally deprived children," primarily through compensatory programs for the poor. In his comments on the legislation, Lyndon Johnson emphasized how basic equality of educational opportunity was to the antipoverty campaign.

Sec. 201. In recognition of the special educational needs of children of low-income families and the impact that concentrations of low-income families have on the ability of local educational agencies to support adequate educational programs, the Congress hereby declares it to be the policy of the United States to provide financial assistance (as set forth in this title) to local educational agencies serving areas with concentrations of children from low-income families to expand and improve their educational programs by various means (including preschool programs) which contribute particularly to meet-

Source: Public Law 89-10 (April 11,1965); Lyndon B. Johnson, *Public Papers of the Presidents of the United States, 1965* (Washington, D.C.: U.S. Government Printing Office, 1966), bk. 1, pp. 407–408.

ing the special educational needs of educationally deprived children. . . .

Sec. 205. (a) A local educational agency may receive a
basic grant or a special incentive grant under this title for
any fiscal year only upon application therefore approved
by the appropriate State educational agency, upon its determination (consistent with such basic criteria as the
Commissioner may establish) —

   (1) that payments under this title will be used for
   programs and projects (including the acquisition of
   equipment and where necessary construction of school
   facilities) (A) which are designed to meet the special
   educational needs of educationally deprived children in
   school attendance areas having high concentrations of
   children from low-income families and (B) which are of
   sufficient size, scope, and quality to give reasonable
   promise of substantial progress toward meeting those
   needs, and nothing herein shall be deemed to preclude
   two or more local educational agencies from entering
   into agreements, at their option, for carrying out joint-
   ly operated programs and projects under this title;

   (2) that, to the extent consistent with the number of
   educationally deprived children in the school district of
   the local educational agency who are enrolled in private
   elementary and secondary schools, such agency has
   made provision for including special educational services and arrangements (such as dual enrollment, educational radio and television, and mobile educational
   services and equipment) in which such children can
   participate;

   (3) that the local educational agency has provided
   satisfactory assurance that the control of funds provid-

ed under this title, and title to property derived therefrom, shall be in a public agency for the uses and purposes provided in this title, and that a public agency will administer such funds and property.

REMARKS BY PRESIDENT LYNDON B. JOHNSON FOLLOWING
ENACTMENT OF THE ELEMENTARY AND SECONDARY
EDUCATION BILL, APRIL 9, 1965

Congress has taken the most significant step of this century to provide widespread help to all of America's schoolchildren. I predict that this is just the beginning, the first giant stride toward full educational opportunity for all of our schoolchildren.

This school bill is a wide-reaching bill. It will offer new hope to tens of thousands of youngsters who need attention before they ever enroll in the first grade. It will help five million children of poor families overcome their greatest barrier to progress — poverty. It will put textbooks in now empty hands. It will establish new centers of learning throughout our entire land, and it will do all of this while leaving the control of education in the hands of local citizens.

I don't know of another single piece of legislation that will help so many for so little cost. For every one of the billion dollars that we spend on this program will come back tenfold as school dropouts change to school graduates. A youngster who finishes high school earns over $35,000 more during his lifetime than a school dropout earns. A college graduate earns over $100,000 more during his lifetime than a high school graduate. And beyond the benefit to the economy of more productive citizens is the simple fact that dropouts are the first casualties of our advancing technology.

I am very proud of your House of Representatives and your United States Senate, and I know every American who looks to our future will join me in applauding the historic action that the Congress has just taken. Since 1870, almost a hundred years ago, we have been trying to do what we have just done — pass an elementary school bill for all the children of America.

26. Equality of Educational Opportunity (1966)

Commissioned by the Civil Rights Act of 1964 to review "the lack of availability of equal educational opportunity for individuals by reason of race, color, religion, or national origins," the Coleman Report assessed the relationships between educational resource inputs (e.g., facilities, materials and curricula, teachers) and student educational achievement. In finding that school resources played a relatively minor role in the achievement gap between black and white students and that socioeconomic background had the most significant impact on school achievement, the Report raised controversial questions about the role of schools.

The great majority of American children attend schools that are largely segregated — that is, where almost

Source: James S. Coleman, *Equality of Educational Opportunity* (Washington, D.C.: U.S. Government Printing Office, 1966), pp. 3, 14–22.

all of their fellow students are of the same racial background as they are. Among minority groups, Negroes are
by far the most segregated. . . . More than 65 percent of
all Negro pupils in the 1st grade attend schools that are
between 90 and 100 percent Negro. And 87 percent at
grade 1, and 66 percent at grade 12, attend schools that
are 50 percent or more Negro. In the South, most students attend schools that are 100 percent white or
Negro. . . .

In its desegregation decision of 1954, the Supreme
Court held that separate schools for Negro and white
children are inherently unequal. This survey finds that,
when measured by that yardstick, American public education remains largely unequal in most regions of the
country, including all those where Negroes form any significant proportion of the population. Obviously, however, that is not the only yardstick. . . .

The schools bear many responsibilities. Among the
most important is the teaching of certain intellectual
skills such as reading, writing, calculating, and problem-
solving. One way of assessing the educational opportunity offered by the schools is to measure how well they
perform this task. Standard achievement tests are available to measure these skills, and several such tests were
administered in this survey to pupils at grades 1, 3, 6, 9,
and 12.

These tests do not measure intelligence, nor attitudes,
nor qualities of character. Furthermore, they are not, nor
are they intended to be, "culture-free." Quite the reverse:
they are culture-bound. What they measure are the skills
which are among the most important in our society for
getting a good job and moving up to a better one, and for
full participation in an increasingly technical world. Con-

sequently, a pupil's test results at the end of public school provide a good measure of the range of opportunities open to him as he finishes school — a wide range of choice of jobs or colleges if these skills are very high; a very narrow range that includes only the most menial jobs if these skills are very low. . . .

With some exceptions — notably Oriental Americans — the average minority pupil scores distinctly lower on these tests at every level than the average white pupil. The minority pupils' scores are as much as one standard deviation below the majority pupils' scores in the first grade. At the 12th grade, results of tests in the same verbal and nonverbal skills show that, in every case, the minority scores are *farther below* the majority than are the 1st graders. . . .

For most minority groups, then, and most particularly the Negro, schools provide no opportunity at all for them to overcome this initial deficiency; in fact, they fall farther behind the white majority in the development of several skills which are critical to making a living and participating fully in modern society. Whatever may be the combination of nonschool factors — poverty, community attitudes, low educational level of parents — which put minority children at a disadvantage in verbal and non-verbal skills when they enter the first grade, the fact is the schools have not overcome it. . . .

When one sees that the average score on a verbal achievement test in School X is 55 and School Y is 72, the natural question to ask is: What accounts for the difference?

There are many factors that in combination account for the difference. This analysis concentrates on one cluster of those factors. It attempts to describe what relationship the school's characteristics themselves (libraries, for example, and teachers and laboratories and so on) seem to have to the achievement of majority and minority groups (separately for each group on a nationwide basis, and also for Negro and white pupils in the North and South).

The first finding is that the schools are remarkably similar in the effect they have on the achievement of their pupils when the socioeconomic background of the students is taken into account. It is known that socioeconomic factors bear a strong relation to academic achievement. When these factors are statistically controlled, however, it appears that differences between schools account for only a small fraction of differences in pupil achievement.

The schools *do* differ, however, in the degree of impact they have on the various racial and ethnic groups. The average white student's achievement is less affected by the strength or weakness of his school's facilities, curricula, and teachers than is the average minority pupil's. To put it another way, the achievement of minority pupils depends more on the schools they attend than does the achievement of majority pupils. Thus, 20 percent of the achievement of Negroes in the South is associated with the particular schools they go to, whereas only 10 percent of the achievement of whites in the South is. Except for Oriental Americans, this general result is found for all minorities.

The conclusion can then be drawn that improving the school of a minority pupil will increase his achievement more than will improving the school of a white child increase his. Similarly, the average minority pupil's achievement will suffer more in a school of low quality than will the average white pupil's. In short, whites, and to a lesser extent Oriental Americans, are less affected one way or the other by the quality of their schools than are minority pupils. This indicates that it is for the most disadvantaged children that improvements in school quality will make the most difference in achievement.

All of these results suggest the next question: What are the school characteristics that account for most variation in achievement? In other words, what factors in the school are most important in affecting achievement?

It appears that variations in the facilities and curriculums of the schools account for relatively little variation in pupil achievement insofar as this is measured by standard tests. Again, it is for majority whites that the variations make the least difference; for minorities, they make somewhat more difference. Among the facilities that show some relationship to achievement are several for which minority pupils' schools are less well equipped relative to whites. For example, the existence of science laboratories showed a small but consistent relationship to achievement. . . . Minorities, especially Negroes, are in schools with fewer of these laboratories.

The quality of teachers shows a stronger relationship to pupil achievement. Furthermore, it is progressively greater at higher grades, indicating a cumulative impact of the qualities of teachers in a school on the pupils' achievement. Again, teacher quality is more important for minority pupil achievement than for that of the majority.

It should be noted that many characteristics of teachers were not measured in this survey; therefore, the results are not at all conclusive regarding the specific characteristics of teachers that are most important. Among those measured in the survey, however, those that bear the highest relationship to pupil achievement are first, the teacher's score on the verbal skills test, and then his educational background—both his own level of education and that of his parents. On both of these measures, the level of teachers of minority students, especially Negroes, is lower.

Finally, it appears that a pupil's achievement is strongly related to the educational backgrounds and aspirations of the other students in the school. Only crude measures of these variables were used (principally the proportion of pupils with encyclopedias in the home and the proportion planning to go to college). Analysis indicates, however, the children from a given family background, when put in schools of different social composition, will achieve at quite different levels. This effect is again less for white pupils than for any minority group other than Orientals. Thus, if a white pupil from a home that is strongly and effectively supportive of education is put in a school where most pupils do not come from such homes, his achievement will be little different than if he were in a school composed of others like himself. But if a minority pupil from a home without much educational strength is put with schoolmates with strong educational backgrounds, his achievement is likely to increase.

This general result, taken together with the earlier examinations of school differences, has important implications for equality of educational opportunity. For . . . the principal way in which the school environments of Negroes and whites differ is in the composition of their student bodies, and it turns out that the composition of the student bodies has a strong relationship to the achievement of Negro and other minority pupils.

This analysis has concentrated on the educational opportunities offered by the schools in terms of their student body composition, facilities, curriculums, and teachers. This emphasis, while entirely appropriate as a response to the legislation calling for the survey, nevertheless neglects important factors in the variability between individual pupils within the same school; this variability is roughly four times as large as the variability between schools. For example, a pupil attitude factor, which appears to have a stronger relationship to achievement than do all the "school" factors together, is the extent to which an individual feels that he has some control over his own destiny. . . . The responses of pupils to questions in the survey show that minority pupils, except for Orientals, have far less conviction than whites that they can affect their own environments and futures. When they do, however, their achievement is higher than that of whites who lack that conviction.

Furthermore, while this characteristic shows little relationship to most school factors, it is related, for Negroes, to the proportion of whites in the schools. Those Negroes in schools with a higher proportion of whites have a greater sense of control. Thus such attitudes, which are largely a consequence of a person's experience in the larger society, are not independent of his experience in school.

27. President's Commission on Campus Unrest (1970)

The outbreak of protest and violence on college campuses in the 1960s and early 1970s was a remarkable — and

---

SOURCE: President's Commission on Campus Unrest. *Report* (Washington, D.C.: U.S. Government Printing Office, 1970), pp. 1–4, 7–8, 12–15.

largely unanticipated—event. Why college students, seemingly one of the most advantaged groups in the nation, should be demonstrating and how to respond became heatedly contested questions. This report by a Presidentially appointed commission found the crisis rooted in antagonism to racial injustice and the Vietnam War, in the alienating impersonality of the multiversity, and in the polarization of values among Americans.

The crisis on American campuses has no parallel in the history of the nation. This crisis has roots in divisions of American society as deep as any since the Civil War. The divisions are reflected in violent acts and harsh rhetoric, and in the enmity of those Americans who see themselves as occupying opposing camps. Campus unrest reflects and increases a more profound crisis in the nation as a whole.

This crisis has two components: a crisis of violence and a crisis of understanding. We fear new violence and growing enmity.

On the nation's campuses, and in their neighboring communities, the level of violence has been steadily rising. Students have been killed and injured; civil authorities have been killed and injured; bystanders have been killed and injured. Valuable public and private property and scholarly products have been burned.

Too many Americans have begun to justify violence as a means of effecting change or safeguarding traditions. Too many have forgotten the values and sense of shared humanity that unite us. Campus violence reflects this national condition.

Much of the nation is so polarized that on many campuses a major domestic conflict or an unpopular initiative in foreign policy could trigger further violent protest and, in its wake, counterviolence and repression.

The Constitution protects the freedom of all citizens to dissent and to engage in nonviolent protest. Dissent is a healthy sign of freedom and a protection against stagnation. But the right to dissent is not the right to resort to violence.

Equally, to respond to peaceful protest with repression and brutal tactics is dangerously unwise. It makes extremists of moderates, deepens the divisions in the nation, and increases the chances that future protest will be violent. . . .

Campus protest has been focused on three major questions: racial injustice, war, and the university itself.

The first issue is the unfulfilled promise of full justice and dignity for Blacks and other minorities. Blacks, like many others of different races and ethnic origins, are demanding today that the pledges of the Declaration of Independence and the Emancipation Proclamation be fulfilled now. Full social justice and dignity—an end to racism in all its human, social, and cultural forms—is a central demand of today's students—black, brown, and white.

A great majority of students and a majority of their elders oppose the Indochina war. Many believe it entirely immoral. And if the war is wrong, students insist, then so are all policies and practices that support it, from the draft to military research, from ROTC to recruiting for defense industry. This opposition has led to an ever-widening wave of student protests.

The shortcomings of the American university are the third target of student protest. The goals, values, administration, and the curriculum of the modern university have been sharply criticized by many students. Students complain that their studies are irrelevant to the social problems that concern them. They want to shape their own personal and common lives, but find the university restrictive. They seek a community of companions and scholars, but find an impersonal multiversity. And they denounce the university's relationship to the war and to discriminatory racial practices.

Behind the student protest on these issues and the crisis of violence to which they have contributed lies the more basic crisis of understanding.

Americans have never shared a single culture, a single philosophy, or a single religion. But in most periods of our history, we have shared many common values, common sympathies, and a common dedication to a system of government which protects our diversity.

We are now in grave danger of losing what is common among us through growing intolerance of opposing views on issues and of diversity itself. . . .

The university, and particularly the faculty, must recognize that the expansion of higher education and the emergence of the new youth culture have changed the makeup and concerns of today's student population. The university should adapt itself to these new conditions. We urge that the university make its teaching programs, degree structure, and transfer and leave policies more flexible and more varied in order to enhance the quality and voluntariness of university study.

We call upon all members of the university to reaffirm that the proper functions of the university are teaching and learning, research and scholarship. An academic community best serves itself, the country, and every principle to which it is devoted by concentrating on these tasks.

Academic institutions must be free—free from outside

interference, and free from internal intimidation. Far too many people who should know better—both within university communities and outside them—have forgotten this first principle of academic freedom. The pursuit of knowledge cannot continue without the free exchange of ideas.

Obviously, all members of the academic community, as individuals, should be free to participate actively in whatever campaigns or causes they choose. But universities as institutions must remain politically neutral except in those rare cases in which their own integrity, educational purpose, or preservation is at stake.

One of the most valid criticisms of many universities is that their faculties have become so involved in outside research that their commitment to teaching seems compromised. We urge universities and faculty members to reduce their outside service commitments. We recognize that alternative sources of university funding will have to be developed to take the place of the money attached to these outside commitments. Realistically, this will mean more unrestricted government aid to higher education. . . .

Students should not expect their own views, even if held with great moral intensity, automatically and immediately to determine national policy. The rhetorical commitment to democracy by students must be matched by an awareness of the central role of majority rule in a democratic society and by an equal commitment to techniques of persuasion within the political process.

The Commission has been impressed and moved by the idealism and commitment of American youth. But this extraordinary commitment brings with it extraordinary obligations: to learn from our nation's past experience, to

recognize the humanity of those with whom they dis-
agree, and to maintain their respect for the rule of law.
The fight for change and justice is the good fight; to drop
out or strike out at the first sign of failure is to insure that
change will never come.

This Commission is only too aware of America's shortcomings. Yet we are also a nation of enduring strength.
Millions of Americans — generations past and present —
have given their vision, their energy, and their patient
labor to make us a more just nation and a more humane
people. We who seek to change America today build on
their accomplishments and enjoy the freedoms they won
for us. It is a considerable inheritance; we must not
squander or destroy it.

28. Open Education (1971)

*Few pedagogical innovations received more attention in
the late sixties and early seventies than "open education."
Heavily influenced by British infant school methods, described below, informal education was a way to break
down the rigid barriers of curriculum and teaching to
engage children more effectively in their own learning.*

Primary schools in Britain divide into "infant" and
"junior" schools. The infant schools in England take the
children from the age of five to seven, and in some

Source: Joseph Featherstone, *Schools Where Children Learn*
(New York: Liveright, 1971), pp. 9–13, 17–18. Selections are reprinted
with the permission of the author and Liveright Publishing Corpora-
tion. Copyright © 1971 by Joseph Featherstone.

authorities, eight. It is in the infant schools that people learn to read and write and to work with numbers. Junior schools take children from seven or eight to eleven, and in some places twelve; they then go on to secondary school. . . .

Westfield Infant School, for example, is a one-story structure, like any of a thousand American buildings, on a working-class housing estate in Leicestershire. If you arrive early, you find a number of children already inside, reading, writing, painting, playing music, tending to pets. Teachers sift in slowly and begin working with students. Apart from a religious assembly (required by law), it's hard to say just when school actually begins because there is very little organized activity for a whole class. The puzzled visitor sees some small group work in mathematics ("maths") or reading, but mostly children are on their own, moving about and talking quite freely. The teacher sometimes sits at her desk, and the children flock to her for consultations, but more often she moves about the room, advising on projects, listening to children read, asking questions, giving words, talking, sometimes prodding.

The hallways, which are about the size of those in American schools, are filled with busy children, displays of paintings and graphs, a grocery store where children use play money and learn to count, easels, tables for collections of shells and plants, workbenches on which to pound and hammer nails and boards, big wooden boxes full of building blocks. . . .

The rooms are fairly noisy—more noisy than many American teachers or principals would allow—because children can talk freely. Sometimes the teacher has to ask for quiet. With as many as forty in some classes, rooms are crowded and accidents happen. Paint spills, a tub overflows, and there are recriminations. Usually the children mop up and work resumes.

The visitor is dazed by the amount and variety and fluency of free writing produced: stories, free-verse poems with intricate images, precise accounts of experiments in "maths" and, finally, looking over a tiny little girl's shoulder, he finds: "Today we had visitors from America. . . . "

After a time, you overcome your confusion at the sheer variety of it all, and you begin making more definite observations. The physical layout of the classrooms is markedly different. American teachers are coming to appreciate the importance of a flexible room, but even in good elementary schools in the United States this usually means having movable, rather than fixed, desks. In the Westfield School there are no individual desks and no assigned places. Around the room (which is about the size of one you would find in an average American school) there are different tables for different activities: art, water and sand play, number work. The number tables have all kinds of number lines — strips of paper with numbers marked on them in sequence; on these children learn to count and reason mathematically. There are beads, buttons, and odd things to count; weights and balances; dry and liquid measures; and a rich variety of apparatus for learning basic mathemetical concepts, some of it homemade, some ready-made. The best of the commercial materials are familiar: Cuisenaire rods, the Dienes multibase material, Stern rods, and attribute or logical blocks. This sort of thing is stressed much more than formal arithmetic. . . .

Gradually it becomes clear how the day proceeds in one

of these rooms. In many infant and some junior schools the choice of the day's routine is left completely up to the teacher; the teacher, in turn, leaves options open to the children. Classes for young children are reaching a point in many schools where there is no real difference between one subject in the curriculum and another, or even between work and play. A school day run on these lines is called, variously, the "free day," the "integrated curriculum," or the "integrated day." The term scarcely matters.

In a school that operates on the integrated day, the teacher usually starts the morning by listing the different activities available. A good deal of material is needed, according to the teachers, but the best of it is often homemade; in any case, it isn't necessary to have thirty or forty sets of everything, because most activities are for a limited number of people. "Six Children Can Play in the Wendy House," says a sign in one classroom. The ground rules are that they must clean up when they finish and they mustn't bother others.

A child might spend the day on his first choice, or he might not. Many teachers confess they get nervous if everybody doesn't do some reading and writing every day; others are committed in principle to letting children choose freely. In practice, many teachers give work when they think it's needed. In this, as in any other way of doing things, teachers tailor their styles to their own temperaments and to those of the children. But the extent to which the children really have a choice and really work purposefully is astonishing. . . .

Formal classroom teaching — the instructor standing up front, talking to the group, or even the first-grade room divided up into reading groups which the teacher listens to separately as she tries desperately to keep order — has disappeared because it imposes a single pattern of learning on a whole group of children (thus forcing the schools to "track," or to group classes by ability), because it ignores the extent to which children teach each other, and because in many workaday schools other methods are proving to be better. Ordinary, formally trained teachers take to the new role when they can see with their own eyes that the result is not chaos.

These methods mean more work for the teacher, not less. In informal conditions, it is essential for the teacher to keep detailed and accurate accounts of what a child is learning, even though at any given moment she might not know what he's up to. Children help by keeping their own records: in some schools they have private shelves where they store writing books, accounts of experiments and work in "maths," lists of the books they've read, and dates when they checked in with the teacher to read aloud. If American parents could see some of the detailed folders of each child's work, including samples of his art work, they would feel, quite rightly, that a report card is a swindle.

When the class seldom meets as a unit, when children work independently, discipline is less of a problem. It does not disappear as a problem, but it becomes less paramount. The purposeful self-discipline of these children is, we were told, just as surprising to middle-aged Englishmen as it is to Americans. It is a recent development, and by no means the product of luck; much hard work and thought go into the arrangement of these classrooms and their materials. When they work at it, teachers find they can make time during the day for children who need it. "I can give all my attention to a child for five minutes, and that's worth more to him than being part of a sea of faces all day," said a teacher in an East London school overlooking the docks. Other teachers say they can watch children as they work and ask them questions; there is a better chance of finding out what children really understand.

29. Prohibition of Sex Discrimination (1972)

In 1972, Congress extended the provision of the Civil Rights Act to preclude discrimination by educational institutions on the basis of gender. The legislation was an early step in efforts to define what constitutes gender discrimination and to extend protection against discrimination to a variety of institutions and situations.

Sec. 901. (a) No person in the United States shall, on the basis of sex, be excluded from participation in, be denied the benefits of, or be subjected to discrimination under any education program or activity receiving Federal financial assistance, except that:

(1) in regard to admissions to educational institutions, this section shall apply only to institutions of vocational education, professional education, and graduate higher education, and to public institutions of undergraduate higher education;

(2) in regard to admissions to educational institutions, this section shall not apply (A) for one year from the date of enactment of this Act, nor for six years after such date in the case of an educational institution

SOURCE: Public Law 92-318 (June 23, 1972).

which has begun the process of changing from being an institution which admits only students of one sex to being an institution which admits students of both sexes, but only if it is carrying out a plan for such a change which is approved by the Commissioner of Education. . . .

(3) this section shall not apply to an educational institution which is controlled by a religious organization if the application of this subsection would not be consistent with the religious tenets of such organization;

(4) this section shall not apply to an educational institution whose primary purpose is the training of individuals for the military services of the United States, or the merchant marine; and

(5) in regard to admissions this section shall not apply to any public institution of undergraduate higher education which is an institution that traditionally and continually from its establishment has had a policy of admitting only students of one sex.

(b) Nothing contained in subsection (a) of this section shall be interpreted to require any educational institution to grant preferential or disparate treatment to the members of one sex on account of an imbalance which may exist with respect to the total number or percentage of persons of that sex participating in or receiving the benefits of any federally supported program or activity, in comparison with the total number or percentage of persons of that sex in any community, State, section, or other area.

30. Bilingual Education (1974)

This revision of the 1968 Bilingual Education Act expanded the federal government's commitment to bilingual programs to include all children of limited English-speaking ability. The Act (and a subsequent revision in 1978) fueled controversy about the purposes and effects of bilingual education, especially over whether programs should seek to maintain non-English languages and cultures or be designed to speed transition to English-speaking classrooms, and whether bilingual education enhanced or retarded school achievement.

Sec. 702. (a) Recognizing—

(1) that there are large numbers of children of limited English-speaking ability;

(2) that many of such children have a cultural heritage which differs from that of English-speaking persons;

(3) that a primary means by which a child learns is through the use of such child's language and cultural heritage;

(4) that, therefore, large numbers of children of limited English-speaking ability have educational needs which can be met by the use of bilingual educational methods and techniques; and

Source: Public Law 93-380-Aug. 21, 1974 (Amended Title VII of the Elementary and Secondary Education Act of 1965).

(5) that, in addition, children of limited English-speaking ability benefit through the fullest utilization of multiple language and cultural resources;

the Congress declares it to be the policy of the United States, in order to establish equal educational opportunity for all children (A) to encourage the establishment and operation, where appropriate, of educational programs using bilingual educational practices, techniques, and methods, and (B) for that purpose, to provide financial assistance to local educational agencies, and to State educational agencies for certain purposes, in order to enable such local educational agencies to develop and carry out such programs in elementary and secondary schools, including activities at the preschool level, which are designed to meet the educational needs of such children; and to demonstrate effective ways of providing, for children of limited English-speaking ability, instruction designed to enable them, while using their native language, to achieve competence in the English language.

Sec. 703. (a) The following definitions shall apply to the terms used in this title:

(1) The term 'limited English-speaking ability,' when used with reference to an individual, means—

(A) individuals who were not born in the United States or whose native language is a language other than English, and

(B) individuals who come from environments where a language other than English is dominant, as further defined by the Commissioner by regulations; and, by reason thereof, have difficulty speaking and understanding instruction in the English language. . . .

(4) (A) The term 'program of bilingual education' means a program of instruction, designed for children of limited English-speaking ability in elementary or secondary schools, in which, with respect to the years of study to which such program is applicable—

(i) there is instruction given in, and study of, English and, to the extent necessary to allow a child to progress effectively through the educational system, the native language of the children of limited English-speaking ability, and such instruction is given with appreciation for the cultural heritage of such children, and, with respect to elementary school instruction, such instruction shall, to the extent necessary, be in all courses or subjects of study which will allow a child to progress effectively through the educational system.

31. Education for All Handicapped Children (1975)

The Education for All Handicapped Children Act of 1975 dramatically expanded the federal government's role in securing educational opportunity for a minority group. The legislation's most provocative sections required that handicapped students be taught, "to the maximum extent appropriate," in the same classrooms with non-handicapped students and that every handicapped student be provided with an individualized education program.

SOURCE: Public Law 94-142 (November 29, 1975).

The Congress finds that —

(1) there are more than eight million handicapped children in the United States today;

(2) the special educational needs of such children are not being fully met;

(3) more than half of the handicapped children in the United States do not receive appropriate educational services which would enable them to have full equality of opportunity;

(4) one million of the handicapped children in the United States are excluded entirely from the public school system and will not go through the educational process with their peers;

(5) there are many handicapped children throughout the United States participating in regular school programs whose handicaps prevent them from having a successful educational experience because their handicaps are undetected;

(6) because of the lack of adequate services within the public school system, families are often forced to find services outside of the public school system, often at great distance from their residence and at their own expense;

(7) developments in the training of teachers and in diagnostic and instructional procedures and methods have advanced to the point that, given appropriate funding, State and local educational agencies can and will provide effective special education and related services to meet the needs of handicapped children;

(8) State and local educational agencies have a responsibility to provide education for all handicapped children, but present financial resources are inadequate to meet the special educational needs of handicapped children; and

(9) it is in the national interest that the Federal Government assist State and local efforts to provide programs to meet the educational needs of handicapped children in order to assure equal protection of the law.

It is the purpose of this Act to assure that all handicapped children have available to them . . . a free appropriate public education which emphasizes special education and related services designed to meet their unique needs, to assure that the rights of handicapped children and their parents or guardians are protected, to assist States and localities to provide for the education of all handicapped children, and to assess and assure the effectiveness of efforts to educate handicapped children. . . .

The State has established . . . procedures to assure that, to the maximum extent appropriate, handicapped children, including children in public or private institutions or other care facilities, are educated with children who are not handicapped, and that special classes, separate schooling, or other removal of handicapped children from the regular educational environment occurs only when the nature of severity of the handicap is such that education in regular classes with the use of supplementary aids and services cannot be achieved satisfactorily, and procedures to assure that testing and evaluation materials and procedures utilized for the purposes of evaluation and placement of handicapped children will be selected and administered so as not to be racially or culturally discriminatory. Such materials or procedures shall be provided and administered in the child's native language or mode of communication, unless it clearly is not feasible to do so, and no single procedure shall be the sole criterion for determining an appropriate educational program for a child.

32. The Scholastic Aptitude Test (1977)

Among the most commonly cited evidence that educational quality had deteriorated was the decline in Scholastic Aptitude Test scores since the mid-1960s. This report, sponsored by the College Board and the Educational Testing Service, probes the phenomenon of declining scores and finds two kinds of causes: new populations taking the examination and educational and social changes that inhibited test achievement.

Every year, for 14 years now, there has been a drop in the average scores more than a million high school juniors and seniors get on the Scholastic Aptitude Test (SAT) they take in seeking admission to college. . . .

Our assessment of this continuous 14-year drop in averages is that it is unquestionably significant. Particularly when the SAT record is set beside the broader pattern of comparable declines on other standardized academic tests, it emerges as a development warranting careful attention by educators and by everybody interested in education. . . .

In general, the causal factors apparently involved here fall into two categories so different that it seems helpful

SOURCE: College Entrance Examination Board, *On Further Examination: Report of the Advisory Panel on the Scholastic Aptitude Test Score Decline* (New York: College Entrance Examination Board, 1977), pp. 1, 44-48. © 1977 by College Entrance Examination Board, New York. Reprinted with permission.

to think in terms of what are virtually two score declines. One reflects primarily changes in the SAT-taking population; these score averages measure a different and broader cross section of American youth from the group they measured 20 or 15 or even 10 years ago. The reasons for the other aspect of the decline are more elusive; they include the apparently pervasive influences, affecting virtually all groups of students alike, of changes in the practices of the schools and in the American social fabric.

Most — probably two-thirds to three-fourths — of the SAT score decline between 1963 and about 1970 was related to the "compositional" changes in the group of students taking this college entrance examination.

That was a period of major expansion in the number and proportion of students completing high school, resulting only in part from the post–World War II population wave, which came along then. The rest of the growth reflected the deliberate national undertaking during that period to expand and extend educational opportunity — by reducing the high school drop-out rate, by trying to eliminate previous discrimination based on ethnicity or sex or family financial circumstance, and by opening college doors much wider. . . .

From about 1970 on, the composition of the SAT-taking population has become comparatively more stabilized with respect to its economic, ethnic, and social background. Yet the score decline continued and then accelerated; there were particularly sharp drops during the three-year period from 1972 to 1975. Only about a quarter of the decline since 1970 can be attributed to continuing change in the make-up of the test-taking group. With a handful of exceptions, the drop in scores in recent years has been virtually across the board, affecting high-scoring and lower-scoring groups alike.

This second set of factors contributing to the SAT score decline can be summarized only in broad terms and with full recognition of two related qualifications. First, any attempt to isolate developments in the schools from those in the society at large turns out to reflect principally the inclination to institutionalize blame for whatever is going wrong; the formal part of the learning process cannot be separated from its societal context. Second, to the extent these causal factors are understood at present, they are inextricably interwoven with each other; any pointing to one development or another as if it were *the*, or even *a*, cause of the decline is invariably misleading.

As already noted, we think that two-thirds to three-quarters of the score decline from 1963 to 1970 and about a quarter of the decline since 1970 were caused by complex interacting factors relating to the changing membership in the population tested. Overall this suggests that about half of the decline is properly traced to these factors. The remainder seems to us identifiable in large part with six other sets of developments:

ONE. There has been a significant dispersal of learning activities and emphasis in the schools, reflected particularly in the adding of many elective courses and a reduction of the number of courses that all students alike are required to take. This has been true particularly in the English and verbal skills area.

TWO. There is clearly observable evidence of diminished seriousness of purpose and attention to mastery of skills and knowledge in the learning process as it proceeds in the schools, the home, and the society generally. This takes a variety of apparently disparate but actually interrelated forms: automatic grade-to-grade promotions, grade inflation, the tolerance of increased absenteeism, the lowering of the demand levels of textbooks and other teaching and learning materials, the reduction of homework, the lowering of college entrance standards, and the inclusion of "remedial" courses in postsecondary education.

Each of these problems has developed in response to the wider spectrum of interests and abilities the schools and colleges are now trying to serve. In a sense the schools may have tried so hard to accommodate the special needs of new and unfamiliar students that these very students along with others have been ill served by not being held to demanding expectations of performance. The lowering of teaching sights is the wrong answer to whatever may have been the consequences of the expansion and extension of educational opportunity. The only right answer is to vary the instructional process still more to take account of increased individual differences, but without lowering standards — which we recognize as a form of magic, but one that has been performed in this country for a long time.

THREE. Particularly because of the impact of television, but as a consequence of other developments as well, a good deal more of most children's learning now develops through viewing and listening than through traditional modes. . . . We surmise that the extensive time consumed by television detracts from homework, competes with schooling more generally, and has contributed to the decline in SAT score averages. . . .

FOUR. There have unquestionably been changes, during the period relating to the score decline, in the role of the family in the educational process. Social sensitivity has precluded thorough inquiry into this area, so that only the readily observable structural changes can be noted: the rapidly increasing number and percentage of children, for example, in less than complete families. While evidence is not available to determine the effect of these changes on students' college entrance examination scores, our conjecture is that it is negative.

FIVE. The concentration of the score declines in the three-year period between 1972 and 1975 leads the panel to suspect strongly that one important element here was the disruption in the life of the country during the time when those groups of test takers were getting ready for their college entrance examinations.

SIX. For whatever combination of reasons, there has been an apparent marked diminution in young people's learning motivation, at least as it appears to be related, directly and indirectly, to their performance on college entrance examinations. Although this may be largely only another dimension of the preceding points, it is perhaps most significant of all that during the past 10 years the curve of the SAT scores has followed very closely the curve of the entire nation's spirits and self-esteem and sense of purpose.

So there is no *one* cause of the SAT score decline, at least as far as we can discern, and we suspect no single pattern of causes. Learning is too much a part of Life to have expected anything else.

5

Dilemmas of the 1980s

33. The Imperative for Educational Excellence (1983)

This report, by the National Commission on Excellence in Education, dramatically set the tone for educational debate in the 1980s. Its condemnation of educational mediocrity and schooling's failure to meet the economic and technological challenges of international competition and the "information age" was quickly taken up in reform efforts to establish excellence in education.

Our Nation is at risk. Our once unchallenged preeminence in commerce, industry, science, and technological innovation is being overtaken by competitors throughout the world. This report is concerned with only one of the many causes and dimensions of the problem, but it is the one that undergirds American prosperity, security, and civility. We report to the American people that while we can take justifiable pride in what our schools and colleges have historically accomplished and contributed to the United States and the well-being of its people, the educational foundations of our society are presently being eroded by a rising tide of mediocrity that threatens our very future as a Nation and a people. What was unimaginable a generation ago has begun to occur—others are matching and surpassing our educational attainments.

SOURCE: National Commission on Excellence in Education, *A Nation at Risk: The Imperative for Educational Reform* (Washington, D.C.: U.S. Government Printing Office, 1983), pp. 5, 18–23.

If an unfriendly foreign power had attempted to impose on America the mediocre educational performance that exists today, we might well have viewed it as an act of war. As it stands, we have allowed this to happen to ourselves. We have even squandered the gains in student achievement made in the wake of the Sputnik challenge. Moreover, we have dismantled essential support systems which helped make those gains possible. We have, in effect, been committing an act of unthinking, unilateral educational disarmament. . . .

We conclude that declines in educational performance are in large part the result of disturbing inadequacies in the way the educational process itself is often conducted. The findings that follow, culled from a much more extensive list, reflect four important aspects of the educational process: content, expectations, time, and teaching.

FINDINGS REGARDING CONTENT

By content we mean the very "stuff" of education, the curriculum. Because of our concern about the curriculum, the Commission examined patterns of courses high school students took in 1964–69 compared with course patterns in 1976–81. On the basis of these analyses we conclude:

Secondary school curricula have been homogenized, diluted, and diffused to the point that they no longer have a central purpose. In effect, we have a cafeteria-style curriculum in which the appetizers and desserts can easily be mistaken for the main course. Students have migrated from vocational and college preparatory programs to "general track" courses in large numbers.

The proportion of students taking a general program of study has increased from 12 percent in 1964 to 42 percent in 1979.

This curricular smorgasbord, combined with extensive student choice, explains a great deal about where we find ourselves today. We offer intermediate algebra, but only 31 percent of our recent high school graduates complete it; we offer French I, but only 13 percent complete it; and we offer geography, but only 16 percent complete it. Calculus is available in schools enrolling about 60 percent of all students, but only 6 percent of all students complete it. . . .

FINDINGS REGARDING EXPECTATIONS

We define expectations in terms of the level of knowledge, abilities, and skills school and college graduates should possess. They also refer to the time, hard work, behavior, self-discipline, and motivation that are essential for high student achievement. . . .

The amount of homework for high school seniors has decreased (two-thirds report less than 1 hour a night) and grades have risen as average student achievement has been declining. In many other industrialized nations, courses in mathematics (other than arithmetic or general mathematics), biology, chemistry, physics, and geography start in grade 6 and are required of all students. The time spent on these subjects, based on class hours, is about three times that spent by even the most science-oriented U.S. students, i.e., those who select 4 years of science and mathematics in secondary schools. . . .

FINDINGS REGARDING TIME

Evidence presented to the Commission demonstrates three disturbing facts about the use that American schools and students make of time: (1) compared to other nations, American students spend much less time on school work; (2) time spent in the classroom and on homework is often used ineffectively; and (3) schools are not doing enough to help students develop either the study skills required to use time well or the willingness to spend more time on school work. . . .

FINDINGS REGARDING TEACHING

The Commission found that not enough of the academically able students are being attracted to teaching; that teacher preparation programs need substantial improvement; that the professional working life of teachers is on the whole unacceptable; and that a serious shortage of teachers exists in key fields.

Too many teachers are being drawn from the bottom quarter of graduating high school and college students. The teacher preparation curriculum is weighted heavily with courses in "educational methods" at the expense of courses in subjects to be taught. A survey of 1,350 institutions training teachers indicated that 41 percent of the time of elementary school teacher candidates is spent in education courses, which reduces the amount of time available for subject matter courses.

The average salary after 12 years of teaching is only $17,000 per year, and many teachers are required to supplement their income with part-time and summer employment. In addition, individual teachers have little influence in such critical professional decisions as, for example, textbook selection.

34. Barriers to Excellence (1985)

The calls for excellence quickly evoked concern that the commitment to equality and equity was being neglected. This report on "children at risk" reaffirmed that commitment and rejected the tendency to pit equality and excellence against one another.

Millions of this nation's children are at risk. This conclusion, emerging from days of public testimony and an extensive review of the literature demands consideration by all citizens, but especially by those responsible for schools and those who establish public policy. While this report gives particular attention to those children who have shared least in the material benefits and economic opportunities of our society, it is ultimately a statement about *all* children and youth and about our society as a whole. . . .

Minority children do not matter as much as non-minority children do to some school officials, judging by the disproportionate numbers of such children who are excluded and underserved by the schools. We know, for example, that Black students are placed in classes for the mildly mentally handicapped at rates more than three

Source: *Barriers to Excellence: Our Children at Risk* (Boston: National Coalition of Advocates for Students, 1985), pp. viii–xiii. Reprinted with permission.

times those of White children. Poor children, too, are
considered less important than non-poor children, if we
contrast the level of financing allocated for their education with that allocated for children in more affluent districts. Non-English-speaking children still face language
and cultural barriers throughout America, and in many
places girls still encounter lower expectations than do
boys.

Differential treatment of children by race, class, sex,
language, and handicap subverts our nation's deepest values of fairness. Such treatment also has enormous practical consequences. In fact, the failure to educate millions
of children is turning the potential for social profit into
grave deficit, the cost of which American taxpayers will
bear both financially and socially, in terms of increased
dependency and the loss of a sense of common purpose. . . .

We reject the implication raised in current public debate that excellence in education for some children can be
made available only at the expense of other children. Indeed, it is our deepest belief that excellence without equity is both impractical and incompatible with the goals of
a democratic society.

We reject the argument, so fashionable today, that all
social programs have failed. Head Start works and should
be expanded to include other eligible children. Compensatory education provided through Title I also reaches
and helps poor children. These programs, however, serve
only a fraction of children of greatest need, and the elements which made them effective, as well as their funding, have been weakened in the last several years. . . .

Based upon our year-long investigation of the schools,
we call for:

- Continued, rather than diminished, federal, state, and local attention to the rights of the disadvantaged and those discriminated against because of race, language, sex, or handicapping condition.
- Greater willingness on the part of those in positions of responsibility to adjust schools to the diverse needs of all students who attend them.
- More democratic governance of all schools which assures parents of a significant role in making decisions about the education of their children and teaches students, by example, principles of democratic participation and the exercise of constitutional rights.
- Establishment of comprehensive early childhood education, day care programs, and in-school support services for children and youth as a means of preventing school failure.
- Enactment of more equitable and adequate systems for financing schools, so that the quality of education available does not depend upon where a child lives.
- More systematic attention to the problems of jobs for youth and dropouts by federal, state, and local education authorities.